Tiger Woods

ATHLETE

Black Americans of Achievement

LEGACY EDITION

Muhammad Ali
Maya Angelou
Josephine Baker
George Washington Carver
Ray Charles
Johnnie Cochran
Frederick Douglass
W.E.B. Du Bois
Jamie Foxx
Marcus Garvey
Savion Glover
Alex Haley
Jimi Hendrix
Gregory Hines
Langston Hughes
Jesse Jackson
Scott Joplin
Coretta Scott King
Martin Luther King, Jr.
Spike Lee
Malcolm X
Bob Marley
Thurgood Marshall
Barack Obama
Jesse Owens
Rosa Parks
Colin Powell
Condoleezza Rice
Chris Rock
Clarence Thomas
Sojourner Truth
Harriet Tubman
Nat Turner
Madam C.J. Walker
Booker T. Washington
Oprah Winfrey
Tiger Woods

Black Americans of Achievement
LEGACY EDITION

Tiger Woods

ATHLETE

Judy L. Hasday

CHELSEA HOUSE
PUBLISHERS
An imprint of Infobase Publishing

Tiger Woods

Chelsea House
An imprint of Infobase Publishing
132 West 31st Street
New York NY 10001

Library of Congress Cataloging-in-Publication Data

Hasday, Judy L., 1957-
 Tiger Woods : athlete / by Judy L. Hasday.
   p. cm. — (Black Americans of achievement : legacy edition)
 Includes bibliographical references and index.
 ISBN 978-0-7910-9714-4 (hardcover)— ISBN 978-1-60413-327-1 (pbk.)
 1. Woods, Tiger. 2. Golfers—United States—Biography. I. Title. II. Series.

 GV964.W66H37 2008
 796.352092—dc22
 [B]   2008018756

Chelsea House books are available at special discounts when purchased in bulk quantities for businesses, associations, institutions, or sales promotions. Please call our Special Sales Department in New York at (212) 967-8800 or (800) 322-8755.

You can find Chelsea House on the World Wide Web at
 http://www.chelseahouse.com

Series design by Keith Trego
Cover design by Keith Trego and Jooyoung An

Printed in the United States of America

Bang ML 10 9 8 7 6 5 4 3 2 1

This book is printed on acid-free paper.

All links and web addresses were checked and verified to be correct at the time of publication. Because of the dynamic nature of the web, some addresses and links may have changed since publication and may no longer be valid.

Contents

The Toughest Loss

Earl Woods was everything to his son, Eldrick "Tiger" Woods: father, mentor, teacher, role model, and best friend. Tiger and his dad forged such a close bond so early in his life that Tiger wanted to play golf just so he could spend time with Earl. Besides, golf was fun. Tiger loved to compete with Earl and wanted to beat him at his favorite game. In the foreword of his father's 1997 book, *Training a Tiger: A Father's Guide to Raising a Winner in Both Golf and Life*, Tiger wrote, "In retrospect, golf for me was an apparent attempt to emulate the person I looked up to more than anyone: my father. He was instrumental in helping me develop the drive to achieve, but his role—as well as my mother's—was one of support and guidance, not interference." Who could have imagined that Tiger's desire to be like his father would help him become one of the greatest golfers in the history of the game?

Tiger Woods (right) practices his putting on the eighth green of the Spyglass Hill Golf Course as his father, Earl Woods, looks on. The father-son pair played as a team for the AT&T Pebble Beach National Pro-Am at Spyglass Hill in January 1998.

A complete understanding of the relationship between Earl Woods and Tiger Woods requires a little bit of background knowledge. Earl Woods was a man worthy of respect and admiration. Although he looked African American, he was also one-quarter Native American and one-quarter Chinese. He was proud of his multiethnic heritage and never let racism prevent him from doing what he wanted to do. The youngest of six children, Earl was born on March 5, 1932, a tough time in history for many people, not just black Americans. His parents were a stonemason named Miles and his wife, Maude Ellen. They lived in Manhattan, Kansas, a town where blacks felt the impact of discrimination, although not as overtly as the violence and racism endured by blacks in the South.

The Woodses taught their son that it was important to work hard and put forward one's best effort. In an interview with Guy Yocum in the February 2004 issue of *Golf Digest*, Earl Woods explained,

> My mother told me I was as good as anybody else, but to have an equal chance, I'd have to do better than the next person. She told me never to judge anybody, to devote myself to being proactive, positive and constructive. That's how I've run my life, and as a result I haven't had time to feel bitter or hostile about the inequities associated with being a black man in America.

NO FUTURE IN BASEBALL

Although Earl Woods had developed a passion for golf by the time Tiger was born, as a young man, baseball was Earl's first love. Besides, the only golf course in Manhattan did not permit blacks to play. Until 1947, blacks were not permitted to play baseball in the major leagues, but that did not stop blacks from playing the game. They played in the Negro Leagues, where some of the greatest ball players in history—including Satchel Paige, Roy Campanella, Josh Gibson, and Cool Papa Bell—competed. In small towns all over the country in the 1940s, white teams played against black teams in exhibition games. When Earl Woods was 11, Roy Campanella and Satchel Paige came through Manhattan on one of their tours of the country. Earl was a pretty good catcher and asked Campanella if he could catch for Paige while he warmed up. Earl Woods later told Yocum of *Golf Digest* what happened:

> He handed me his mitt and said, "Don't hurt yourself, boy." I said, "Don't worry. I've got a major-league arm." Campanella giggled at that. I said, "By the way, tell Satch that after he throws his last pitch, he'd better duck, because I'm gonna throw the ball right through his chest. Roy just

shook his head. Satch's first pitch came in real easy. I threw
it back harder than he threw it to me. Satch threw the next
one harder. So did I. By the time he threw his last warm-
up pitch, he was really bringing it. And when I caught it, I

Satchel Paige: "The Best I've Ever Faced"

Baseball great Joe DiMaggio once called Satchel Paige "the best I've ever
faced, and the fastest." Paige's remarkable skills on the mound helped fill
ballparks and made baseball fans come to games, even during the Depres-
sion.

Satchel Paige's athletic skills were matched only by his showmanship. He
named his pitches: the Long Tom, the bee ball, the four-day creeper, the trouble ball, the two-hump blooper, the hurry-up ball. One of his more dazzling
throws was the hesitation pitch, delivered only after he intentionally paused
before throwing as his left foot touched the ground. He sometimes waved in
his outfielders to sit behind the pitcher's mound while he struck out a batter.
Perhaps more astounding than his theatrics was his longevity: He played
consistently from 1926 to 1957 in the Negro Leagues, then in Major League
baseball, and finally in a stint with the Miami Marlins (a Philadelphia Phillies
triple-A farm team). He still pitched from time to time during the 1960s.

Leroy "Satchel" Paige was probably born on July 7, 1906 (the date has
never been definitively confirmed) in Mobile, Alabama. He was the sixth of
the 12 children of John Paige, a gardener, and his wife, Lula Coleman. By the
time he was a teen, Leroy was sent to reform school for truancy and shop-
lifting, but while he was there, he decided he would pitch baseballs rather
than throw rocks. He reportedly earned his nickname as a baggage porter
in Mobile, where he could carry so many bags (satchels) at one time that he
resembled a "satchel tree."

Paige began his athletic career with the Chattanooga Black Lookouts in
the Negro Southern League in 1926. He played with at least seven other
Negro League teams over the next 24 years, including the Pittsburgh Craw-
fords (1931–1937), where he established himself as the league's premier
pitcher. During his tenure with the team, he also played for the Kansas City
Monarchs (1935–1936) and the Santo Domingo All-Stars (1937). Paige
racked up a 31-4 record in 1933, 64 consecutive scoreless innings,
and a 21-game winning streak during this period. He led the Kansas City
Monarchs (1935–1936, 1939–1948) to four consecutive American League

sprang out of my crouch and threw it right where Satchel's chest was. You better believe he got out of the way. The second baseman caught the ball ankle-high, on the right-hand side of the bag. Roy said, "Boy, you really do have a

pennants and a Negro World Series championship in 1942. On his celebrated exhibition tours, he played with the Negro League All-Stars against competition from the Major League, where he drew the attention of white baseball fans.

Paige achieved his true goal—to play baseball in the Major League—on his birthday in 1948, when Cleveland Indians promoter and owner Bill Veeck signed him up during the pennant race. Now in his forties, Paige was decades older than every other ballplayer in the Major League, and Veeck was accused of using the signing to garner publicity. "If Satch were white," Veeck retorted, "he would have been in the majors 25 years earlier and the question would not have been [raised]." Paige himself never worried about whether he was too old to play ball. "Age is a question of mind over matter," he famously said. "If you don't mind, it doesn't matter."

Just one year earlier, Jackie Robinson had shattered baseball's color barrier when he was moved up to the Brooklyn Dodgers for the start of the 1947 season. Paige became the first African-American pitcher in the American League. Determined to silence his critics, he posted a 6–1 record to help the Cleveland Indians win the pennant. Paige pitched two seasons for the Indians before he joined the St. Louis Browns as a spot starter and relief pitcher. There, he compiled a 12–10 record and represented the Browns in the major league All-Star Game in 1952–1953. During his career in the majors, he posted a 28–31 record with a 3.29 ERA and 32 saves.

Paige continued to barnstorm long after his career in the Major League officially ended. In 1959, he appeared in a United Artists movie, *The Wonderful Country*, starring Robert Mitchum and Julie London. Paige's character, Sgt. Tobe Sutton, was a tough Union army cavalry officer in charge of a segregated black unit. He was extremely proud of his film credit, as he was of his 1962 autobiography (as told to David Lipman), *Maybe I'll Pitch Forever*. He also became the first member of the Negro Leagues to be elected into the Baseball Hall of Fame in 1971. Paige died on June 8, 1982, at his Kansas City home.

major-league arm." I did have a good arm. And I can say that I caught the great Satchel Paige.

Earl's mother emphasized the importance of education to her children. Fortunately, Earl was a gifted athlete and earned a baseball scholarship to Kansas State University. Long before Tiger started to break barriers in the predominantly white sport of golf, Earl was forging his own history as the first black man to play baseball in the old Big 12 Conference. His teammates treated him well, but Earl had to endure the racial discrimination of the time, such as being forced to stay in a separate hotel when the team went on the road. Although Earl's father had dreamed his son would play professional ball for the Kansas City Monarchs in the Negro Leagues, Earl listened to his mother's advice and got an education. He earned his degree in sociology.

ARCHITECT OF A CHAMPION

After college, Earl Woods joined the military rather than take a low-paying job. At that time, discrimination still impeded the ability of blacks to get ahead in a career. Woods also married Barbara Hart and had three children: two sons, Earl Jr. and Kevin, and a daughter, Royce. The military took Woods away from his family for long periods of time, and he was not able to be the kind of father that he would have liked to be. At the end of a 20-year military career, he had completed two tours of duty in Vietnam and attained the rank of lieutenant colonel in the Green Berets. The time spent away from his wife and children had taken its toll on the marriage, however, and the ensuing divorce left him rather estranged from his children, which was something Woods deeply regretted.

When the military sent Woods to Thailand, he met a young Thai woman who captured his attention. Although another marriage was not foremost in his mind, Woods fell in love with Kultida Punsawad. He brought her back to the United States, where they were married in 1969. Woods promised himself he would be a better husband and more attentive father if he and Kultida had any children. When Kultida gave birth to Tiger, Woods kept his promise. Many people have asked Woods about his intentions about his son during the phenomenal rise of Tiger's career. Some in the golf community thought that Woods was only interested in having a golf career vicariously through his son. Others thought that his only focus and intention was to produce a golf champion. They could not have been more wrong. Woods's number-one desire was that Tiger be a good person—a man who would care about others, be respectful, understand the difference between right and wrong, and accept responsibility for the choices he made both as a child and as a man. As MSNBC commentator Jim McCabe wrote in his article "Earl Woods Had a Life of Fulfillment,"

> The world's greatest golfer can take credit for all the major championships he wants, but when it comes to the quality person that he is—the dignified star, the respectful youngster, the cooperative icon—Tiger Woods knows he must give thanks to his parents, Earl and Kultida. They poured the foundation. They showed the way. That Tiger Woods followed in a manner that has helped make him one of the world's most admired athletes is a tribute to the power of love.

As Woods nurtured his son's character, he did so with the heart of a father rather than a coach or manager. He told writer Bill Guttman that he learned to set his priorities when he was given a second chance at fatherhood. "Your priority is the welfare of the child first. Who he is, and what is going into making him a good person, has priority over making him a good athlete." Woods was a good teacher, and the things people say about his son today reflect those teachings. Tiger's first golf coach, Butch Harmon, a long-time friend of Woods's, said that, if you look at Tiger's personality, it is all

Earl Woods's influence. What greater compliment could you earn than to hear from others that your child has the same character, dignity, and moral fiber that you possess?

TO EVERYTHING THERE IS A SEASON

Earl Woods was a successful parent who had brought up a good person. For him, Tiger's superstar athleticism was a fun and enjoyable bonus. When Tiger was born, Woods told his wife that he believed his son was special. Later he was proud of Tiger for his accomplishments on and off the golf course. Earl earned his son's respect and friendship, and they had forged a special and lasting relationship. So when Eldrick "Tiger" Woods had to face the greatest challenge in his young life, it would have made perfect sense to seek his father for his counsel, guidance, and support. Unfortunately, the challenge was not to conquer a golf course or compete for yet another championship among the many he had already added to his professional portfolio. On May 3, 2006, Tiger learned that his mentor, best friend, role model, and father would no longer be cheering him from the gallery. At the age of 74, Earl Woods had passed away early in the morning that day at his home in Cypress, California.

The next day, Tiger was scheduled to play in the Wachovia Championship tournament in Charlotte, North Carolina, but he withdrew. Two of his closest friends on the golf tour, Mark O'Meara and John Cook, also withdrew from the tournament and flew out to California to be with Tiger, his wife, Elin, and his mother, Kultida. On May 5, a private formal service was

IN HIS OWN WORDS...

"I have so many great memories of my dad. He loved golf. I always smile when I think back to my childhood. A lot of my memories of dad come from golf."

held in California, as Earl was buried in his hometown of Manhattan, Kansas. Later that day, invited guests assembled at the Tiger Woods Learning Center in Anaheim for a memorial service and reception to honor Earl's life. Stories and memories of Earl Woods were shared among the more than 200 in attendance, including former basketball star Charles Barkley, PGA Tour commissioner Tim Finchem, Nike chairman Phil Knight, and volleyball player Gabrielle Reece and her husband, professional surfer Laird Hamilton.

The only public acknowledgement from Tiger Woods about the death of his father appeared on his Web site, www.tigerwoods.com. On it he posted the following message:

> I'm very saddened to share the news of my father's passing at home early this morning. My dad was my best friend and greatest role model, and I will miss him deeply. I'm overwhelmed when I think of all of the great things he accomplished in his life. He was an amazing dad, coach, mentor, soldier, husband and friend. I wouldn't be where I am today without him, and I'm honored to continue his legacy of sharing and caring.

Although Earl was no longer around to provide advice to his son, Tiger remembered that his father was adamant about being in tune with himself to know when to play and when not to play. Earl had always counseled Tiger that, if he was not going to be mentally in the game, he was not ready to play. Tiger heeded his father's advice: He did not play golf for nine weeks after Earl's death. Tiger knew that the connection between the game and his father would only remind him that Earl was gone, and he would not be able to concentrate on his golf game.

Tiger did not pick up a club for a month after his father's funeral. He skipped the Memorial Tournament, an event he had not missed since he had entered professional golf 10 years

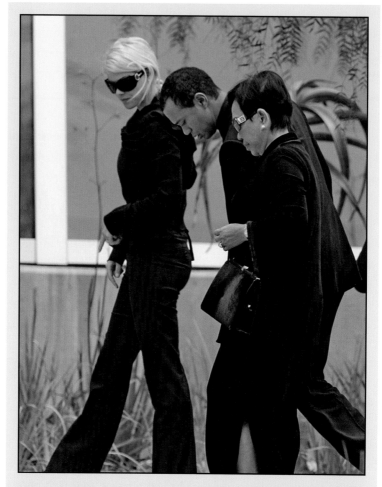

Tiger Woods (center) with wife, Elin Nordegren (left), and his mother, Kultida, arrive at a reception following burial services for Earl Woods. The death of Earl Woods was an emotional loss for Tiger, who had been especially close to his father.

earlier. Fellow golfer Davis Love III understood Tiger's absence well, and he told ESPN writer Bob Harig, "Obviously Tiger is going to be in the same boat as me every time he goes out to play golf," said Love, who lost his father in a 1988 airplane crash. "He'll think of his father. That's not going to change. It'll be hard for a while, but it will also be a positive for him down the road." In early June, Tiger finally resurfaced, and he shot a practice round at Winged Foot (West) Golf Club, site of the 106th U.S. Open Tournament. He felt he was ready to start to play competitive golf again, but he took it slowly at first to get back into his groove. Tiger told *USA Today's* Jerry Potter, "You start back with the fundamentals. That's grip, posture, stance and alignment. Those are the things I learned from dad. As I was working, all those memories came rushing back." Tiger added that he knew his father would want him to go out and play, to give it his best shot.

There was a lot of pressure on Tiger when he stepped up to the first tee on Thursday, June 15, the first round of the U.S. Open. Observers seemed to be focusing on every move he made, every expression on his face, and every word he spoke. The question on everyone's mind was how well Tiger would play. Would his emotions overtake him and interfere with his ability to play golf the way he had for so long? No one had to wait long for the answer. Tiger bogeyed (shot 1 over par, which is the number of strokes designated for a particular hole) the first three holes and ended the day 6 shots over par with a score of 76. Although he improved as the day went on, he posted the same score after Friday's round, and he missed the cut. Anyone within 10 shots of the leader made the cut, and all players who ended the day at 9 over or better moved on. Tiger finished 12 over, which eliminated him from the tournament and marked the first time he had ever missed the cut in a major tournament. In retrospect, Tiger acknowledged that he had not been ready to return to the game. In the *Associated Press* article, *A Tragic, Terrific Year for Tiger*, he was quoted as saying, "It took me longer than I thought to cope with it," Woods said of his father's death. "I've never gone through anything like that."

A RETURN TO GREATNESS

At his next tournament outing in July at the Western Open, Tiger started slow and finished the first round two over par.

Afraid he would miss the cut in his second consecutive tournament, Tiger headed off to the practice range and shot anything and everything for about three hours. When he was through, he felt the burden of his grief lift, and he went on to shoot a 67 the next day. Tiger made a great run to capture the lead, but he finished second overall. It was enough to get him back to his former level of play, when it seemed he could win almost effortlessly. Tiger went on to win his next six tournaments, including two majors, the British Open and the Professional Golfers' Association (PGA) Championship. There are some players who never win six tournaments in their careers, let alone six in one season. Only two other players, Ben Hogan and Byron Nelson, know what it is like to go six for six. If anyone was in doubt, after that kind of finish for the year, Tiger put all doubts to rest. Still, it was an emotion-filled time for him, even as Tiger began to win again. After his win at the British Open on July 23, Tiger threw his hands in the air and screamed "Yes!" as if to release the last of his own internal struggles. He turned to his caddie, Steve Williams, and sobbed on his shoulder as they walked off the eighteenth hole.

Voted AP Male Athlete of the Year and the AP Sports Story of the Year, Tiger Woods experienced the best and worst in 2006. In all, he won eight PGA Tour championships and earned more than $9 million for the year. He continued to pile up statistics for the record books, and he remained the player to beat on the tour. Despite his professional successes, Tiger was quite somber when asked how he felt about 2006: "If you take into account what happened off the golf course, it's my worst year. People asked me . . . 'How do you consider the year?' I consider it as a loss. In the grand scheme of things, golf doesn't even compare to losing a parent." Even after a great professional season, Tiger's answer showed the grace and sense of perspective learned from his father. He could not have paid a greater tribute to Earl Woods, who had indeed reared a good and caring person.

Raising a Tiger

Eldrick "Tiger" Woods was born on December 30, 1975, in Cypress, California. His was just one of the many births recorded that day in the United States; there was nothing unusual to make his arrival unique or newsworthy. It was the last time, however, that Eldrick would blend in as just another child born on that particular day. Even before he could walk, there were hints that he had been born to greatness. His parents, too, displayed qualities out of the ordinary.

Eldrick's father, Earl Woods, had been born in an era when racial discrimination and segregation were accepted practices in America, which could have limited his options as an adult. Although he was multiracial—part black, part Native American, and part Asian—Earl Woods was seen as a black man in a white man's world. He did not let that stop him from earning a scholarship to play baseball as the only black man on a team in an all-white conference. Earl carved out his own barrier-breaking path about the same time that baseball player Jackie Robinson was signed to play with the Brooklyn Dodgers as the first black man in the major league since the game was segregated. Earl Woods went on to have a distinguished military career as a Green Beret, completing two tours of duty in Vietnam and earning the rank of lieutenant colonel before he retired in 1974.

Tiger's mother, Kultida Punsawad, had been born into a family of wealth and prominence thousands of miles from California, in Thailand, a country in southeast Asia that neighbors Myanmar (formerly Burma), Cambodia, and Malaysia. Most of Thailand's population (95 percent) practices the Buddhist religion. Kultida, a Buddhist, followed the customary practices of Thai women, which included having a chaperone accompany her on dates. When Earl Woods met Kultida Punsawad, she was a secretary at the U.S. Army office in Bangkok, the capital city of Thailand. He asked her out, but their first date did not start off on the right foot. Woods said he would meet Punsawad at eight o'clock. After he waited several hours and she did not appear, he thought that she had changed her mind, and he went home to bed. The next morning, Punsawad tracked Woods down and told him she thought they had a date. He told her he had waited long after eight the previous night for her. She told him she had waited for a while after eight in the morning. Woods did not know that Thai women did not go out at night. Punsawad insisted that they still had a date, and with her chaperone in tow, she asked Woods to take her to the Temple of the Reclining Buddha to attend a holy day service. Intrigued by this strong-willed woman, Woods accompanied her to the temple.

HONORING TIGER ONE

Woods and Punsawad fell in love, so when his tour of duty in Thailand was over, Woods asked her to return to the United States with him. They married and settled in Brooklyn, New York, where Woods was assigned to Fort Hamilton. It was there that an officer friend persuaded Woods to play his first game of golf. Although he was already 42 years old and did not do well in his first game, the sport intrigued Woods. In his typical fashion, he practiced and analyzed every stroke and swing, improving so much that within four months he beat his friend by four strokes in a rematch, shooting an 81. Woods played with a 1 handicap within five years. He later told *Golf World* writer Peter McDaniel about that first time on the course, saying, "I got hooked on that round of golf. I realized just what I'd been missing my whole life. I said if I ever have another son I'm starting him out at a young age."

Three months after his return to the United States, Woods retired from the military, and he and his wife moved to Orange County in southern California. There, Woods took a job where he negotiated contracts for materials for a rocket program run by aerospace manufacturer McDonnell Douglas. Kultida Woods was pregnant and Earl Woods wanted to be settled in a house near work before their first child arrived. They both liked a particular neighborhood in Cypress, where the elementary school and a small park were just a few blocks away, and they found a two-bedroom home on a corner lot that they could afford. Unfortunately, the Woods family was not welcomed by the neighbors in this predominantly white section of town. Some pelted the house with overripe limes from the trees that lined the block, and others shot pellets at the windows in an attempt to drive Earl and Kultida Woods from the neighborhood. Earl Woods was not about to be intimidated by the racial attacks against his family, and he did not intend to move. Once it became apparent to the neighbors that their hostile tactics would not work, the attacks stopped.

At Long Beach Hospital on the last Tuesday of December, 1975, Kultida gave birth to a baby boy whom the Woodses named Eldrick. Kultida used the "E" for Earl at the beginning of his name and the "K" for Kultida at the end. Earl knew from the moment his son was born that he would call him "Tiger."

He had two reasons for doing so. While he was stationed in Vietnam, Woods became close friends with a South Vietnamese soldier named Vuong Dang Phong. Phong had saved Woods's life on more than one occasion, and Earl thought his friend fought courageously. As a tribute to Phong's bravery, Woods had nicknamed his friend Tiger. He lost track of Phong after the war, but he always hoped that they would find one another again in later years. Earl gave his son the same nickname because he hoped that he would grow up to be as courageous as his friend Phong. Earl also thought that someday Phong might see the names Tiger and Woods together and make the connection to his long lost buddy. Unfortunately, Phong never knew about Tiger Woods or the honor Earl had bestowed upon him; a search years later turned up a grave outside a relocation camp in North Vietnam. There would be no happy reunion, but Woods gave Phong (whom he referred to as Tiger One) an enduring legacy when he named his son Tiger.

INTRODUCING A GAME

Neither age nor fatherhood had dimmed the passion that Earl Woods felt for golf. Although racism sometimes denied him the opportunity to play the game, he was determined that would not be the case for his son. People played golf at country clubs, which were run and patronized by white men. The professional golf ranks were almost all white men. Despite the "token" black golfers, such as Lee Elder, Charlie Sifford, and Calvin Peete, the sport has always been a white man's game, and it is usually

DID YOU KNOW?

Did you know that Earl and Kultida Woods had to have a child? According to Thai beliefs, it demonstrates that the marriage has been consummated and is therefore legitimate.

At a very young age, Tiger Woods began exhibiting interest in and aptitude for golf. Here is Tiger at 11 months, just one month after he climbed down from his high chair, taking his first swing with a golf club.

impossible to find a black player at a professional tournament. Earl Woods loved the game and wanted to share that love with his son. Even more, he wanted Tiger to be the one to shatter the inequities forever by opening up more opportunities for blacks and other minorities to show that they could play the game just as well as their white counterparts.

Woods loved to have his young son's company while he practiced. He had set up a makeshift practice driving range in his garage, where he used a small piece of carpet in place of a tee-off. He also set up a net to catch the balls he hit. His theory was that a child introduced to a sport at a younger age would develop into a better athlete and master the sport earlier and more successfully than those who began playing later in life. With that in the back of his mind, Woods put six-month-old Tiger in a high chair to watch him while he practiced his swing. As Woods hit each golf ball up into the net, Tiger became mesmerized by his father's actions and agitated by any interruption, including Kultida's attempts to feed him. Finally they reached a compromise: Woods would take a shot, and then Tiger would take a spoonful of the food from his mother. It was the only way Kultida could get Tiger to eat while he was out in the garage and also allow him to see his father hit those balls.

Earl Woods had his theories about early learning, but he never imagined that his son could absorb every nuance, every adjustment, every change he made in his swing or his club grip. He was stunned when he discovered that his son must have been doing just that. One day, when Tiger was 10 months old and could barely walk, he climbed down from his high-chair when Woods sat down in the garage to take a rest from his practice. Although the golf clubs were bigger than he was, Tiger took one in his hands, dropped a ball on the carpet, and even began the waggle to get ready to swing. It was as if Tiger had memorized the entire motion of a tee shot. Woods was absolutely flabbergasted. He ran in the house to get his wife so she could witness what he had just seen his son do. They looked at each other and realized that they might have a child prodigy before them. Although he was still in diapers, still drank milk from a bottle and ate baby food from a jar, Tiger had been able to simulate the golf swing of a seasoned professional. Could Earl Woods cultivate that apparent talent? Was his theory true that kids who began sports at a younger age would develop greater talent? One thing was sure, Woods had the prototype right in front of him in his garage in the form of his son.

3

The Young, Budding Golfer

Tiger was not born in the stance of a golfer, shoulders perpendicular to the ball on the tee, with a golden swing that could launch a tiny ball more than 300 yards (274 meters) down the fairway. Nevertheless, the infant still in diapers watched his father practice in the garage as if his brain were videotaping his father's every move, every nuance of his swing, and how the ball reacted. With the makeshift club Earl Woods adapted for him, Tiger demonstrated the ability to swing through on the ball with the subtle weight shift, speed, balance, and hand-eye coordination of someone born with innate talent. Earl realized that his son had a special and rare talent, and he also knew that a great deal of responsibility came with that realization. In John Strege's *Tiger: A Biography of Tiger Woods*, Earl said,

> It was special. It's a God-given talent. I used to ask, "Why me? What did I do to deserve a kid like this?" It was an

awesome responsibility. At a young impressionable age, the slightest miscalculation on my part could have turned him against golf for the rest of his life. There's a fine line between corrective counseling, coaching, and being a parent. It's not easy when you have a gifted child.

Tiger continued to amaze his parents, demonstrating the focus and attention span of someone much older, as he happily whacked a tennis ball around the house, chased it, then whacked it again, for up to two hours at a time. Still in diapers and 18 months old when he went to his first driving range, Tiger proceeded to empty his bucket of golf balls and hit them with his sawed-off iron club one at a time with an accuracy that amazed those who watched nearby. Earl Woods next took Tiger to the Destroyer Golf Course at the naval base, where he had golf privileges as a retired officer. Setting his son up on the 410-yard (375 meter), par-four hole on the course, Woods gave Tiger the full exposure to the look, feel, smells, and sounds of being on a golf course. Tiger shot an 11 on the hole: 8 shots to get to the green and a 3-putt into the cup. While most children his age were playing in sandboxes, Tiger was practicing swings to get out of bunker sand traps. It was not at all unusual for Tiger to fall asleep in his stroller on the way back to the car after playing golf; once he was home again, he reverted to the toddler he still was, who drank from a bottle and went down for his afternoon nap.

THE TIGER GOES PUBLIC

When Tiger reached the age of two, Kultida Woods decided that her son's skills needed to be made public. She contacted former NFL Green Bay Packers defensive back and Los Angeles-based KCBS-TV sports anchor Jim Hill and suggested that he come to the Navy golf course to see Tiger play a complete hole. Hill was curious about this supposed two-year-old phenomenon, so he took Kultida up on her invitation and arrived with a film

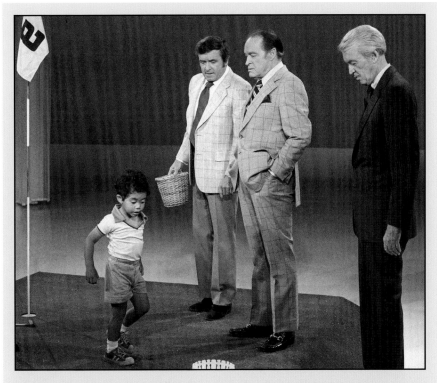

At age two, Tiger made his first appearance on national television when he was invited to be a guest on the *Mike Douglas Show*. Here, Tiger walks across the green as (left to right) host Mike Douglas, comedian Bob Hope, and actor Jimmy Stewart look on.

crew to capture Tiger in action. Hill was truly amazed at what he witnessed. When he aired the piece that night during his report, Hill predicted, "This young man is going to be to golf what Jimmy Connors and Chris Evert are to tennis."

Just as Kultida had planned, others began to notice her son. Tiger's appearance on KCBS-TV caught the eye of one of the producers of the *Mike Douglas Show*, a popular syndicated talk show that featured guests from the arenas of entertainment, business, politics, and sports. Notable appearances included Bette Davis, Billy Joel, Muhammad Ali, and George Burns.

Legendary comedian and entertainer Bob Hope made an appearance on the show on October 6, 1978. Passionate about golf, Hope once said that the sport was his profession and he only told jokes to pay his greens fees. Douglas's producer thought it would be great to have Tiger come on the same show as Hope, so arrangements were made to fly in Earl and Tiger Woods to demonstrate Tiger's golf abilities to Hope and the audience. Dressed in khaki shorts, a polo shirt, and a red baseball cap, Tiger came on stage with his clubs in a miniature golf bag and showed no signs of stage fright. Earl set up a ball on a tee on a small grass-covered platform, gave Tiger his modified driver, and the two-year-old set himself and swung at the ball. He sent the perfect shot flying straight into a backdrop on the stage.

A highly impressed Bob Hope "challenged" Tiger to a putting match, which did not go as well for the youngster as did his driving shot. After he missed three putts, Tiger complained that the green had a huge break (slope) in it. Tiger's comment drew even more attention as a surprised Douglas joked that Tiger could not read a sentence but was able to read the surface of a putting green. Tiger's appearance on the *Mike Douglas Show* was not to be his last appearance on television while still a child. When he was five years old, Tiger was invited to show off his talent on *That's Incredible,* a television show that featured highly unusual or dangerous stunts, feats, and breakthrough successes in medicine. Tiger boldly told cohost Fran Tarkenton that, when he grew up, he was going to beat golf greats Jack Nicklaus and Tom Watson. Then he proceeded to hit a bunch of whiffle balls into the audience. The ease with which Tiger appeared on stage and spoke to Tarkenton demonstrated incredible poise for such a young child. One thing was sure: Tiger was not shy in the spotlight.

It soon became apparent that Tiger was ready to participate in competitions geared toward kids (usually age 10 and younger). At the Navy courses, Tiger played against much older kids and won. When he was just 3 years old, he played against 10- and 11-year-old boys in a "Pitch, Putt, and Drive" tournament and again won. Shortly before his fourth birthday, Tiger shot a score of 48 from the red tees (shortest course length) on the back nine holes of a par-72 Destroyer Course (a score of 36 would have been par on nine holes). He did, however, have one advantage. Instead of having to hit the ball on the fairway, Tiger swung each shot off a tee that his father set up for him because he still did not have the strength to get the ball airborne from the ground. His score would have been great for kids three times his age, which made his accomplishment that much more impressive.

Earl Woods was not aware of how savvy his young prodigy was until four-year-old Tiger walked off the golf course, his pocket full of quarters. Earl asked his son where he got the coins. Tiger replied that he had won them putting on a practice green against a bunch of older boys who were competing in a junior championship tournament. Earl told Tiger he did not want him to putt for quarters anymore. He did not think Tiger realized that he was gambling, only that he won a contest. Still, a few months later Earl caught Tiger as he walked off the gold course with his pockets stuffed with dollar bills. He again asked his son where he got the money, and Tiger replied that he had been playing a skins game. In this golf game, each hole has a value in money or points, and whoever wins the hole (the skin), wins what the skin is worth. Tiger did not understand how he had disobeyed his father, who told him not to putt for quarters. Earl Woods did not want his son to gamble and told him not to play for anything going forward. Of course, he would have to modify that directive once Tiger turned pro and began to earn money for winning tournaments.

LIFE'S HARSHER REALITIES

Tiger may have charmed the public when he demonstrated his phenomenal golf skills at such a young age, but there was

another side of life, one far removed from the fun and ado-
ration that he had not yet experienced. He nearly attained
celebrity status with his television appearances and media
attention, and people mostly saw him as an adorably gifted
child. Some people, however, could not see beyond his color
and they saw him as an upstart black child; these people
injected the ugliness of racism and discrimination into Tiger's
otherwise bright world. Earl and Kultida Woods had already
experienced the malevolence of racism when they moved into
their neighborhood in Cypress, California. Tiger had already
run into problems at some of the golf clubs that told him that
he could not play on their courses without adult supervision
until he was 10. Tiger saw many white children younger than
10 who played unsupervised, but he did not realize that the
real problem was that he was black. He only learned later that
this form of discrimination was wrapped in a less offensive
term: selective enforcement.

For many years, the game of golf had been open only to
white people. Blacks and other minorities had been forbidden
to join country clubs (most of which have golf courses), and
the PGA enforced its whites-only policy until 1961. The first
color-barrier breakthrough in a major golf event did not happen until 1975, the same year Tiger was born. It occurred at
the 39th Annual Masters tournament, one of the most coveted
Majors events on the PGA Tour. It was the first time a black
man, golfer Lee Elder, won an invitation to play at the Augusta
National Golf Club, home of the Masters. Elder's presence was
a start, but it took another 15 years before the Club accepted
its first black member. Not much else had changed about the
integration of the game; it still remained a mostly Caucasian
sport.

Perhaps the biggest trauma of Tiger's young life came when
he went off to kindergarten in the fall of 1981. In a mostly
white neighborhood, it stood to reason that the major-
ity of the school population would also be white, with few

minorities. On Tiger's first day, a group of white boys grabbed him, tied him to a tree, threw stones at him and called him racist names. Although the boys were caught and punished, Tiger was very upset about the incident. Earl Woods knew his son would face far greater difficulties in the world of golf because of his ethnicity, and he tried to impress upon Tiger how essential it was to learn how to ignore name-calling and other forms of ignorance by people. If he did not learn to do that, racism would follow him and interfere with his goals throughout his life.

Earl did his best to prepare his son for whatever obstacles he might face as he worked on his game. Kultida, too, did her part to ensure that Tiger would not be limited by racist attitudes, especially those that made it difficult to play the game that he loved or affected his ability to get a good education. Both aspects of her son's life were important to her, although education came first. Tiger was not allowed to practice or play golf until all of his homework was done. He was an exceptional student and was even recommended to skip a grade. Kultida and Earl Woods discussed the possibility with Tiger, who refused. He explained to his parents that although he had no qualms about competing against older kids in a game of golf, he wanted to stay with kids his own age in school. Earl and Kultida wanted their son to be as well adjusted as possible under the circumstances, so Tiger's choice was fine with them.

THE TAO OF GOLF

Although he handled his extraordinary talent with great maturity, Tiger had occasional flashes of temper not unusual for his age. Sometimes, after making a bad shot, Tiger would throw his club to the ground in frustration. Earl Woods would take his son to task immediately, asking him who was responsible for that bad shot, which gave Tiger a chance to pause and think about it. Tiger would tell his father that he realized that it was all his own responsibility, but that he sometimes had trouble with his temper. Woods understood his young son's frustration. He explained to Tiger that as he got older he could learn to channel his anger into something positive, and that mistakes would only make him come back stronger and do better on his next shot. Thus, in Tiger's golf lesson, Woods also taught his son a life lesson. Tiger would learn that he needed to take responsibility for his actions, which enabled him to see the parallels between the game and life.

While Earl Woods worked with his son to channel that energy into his game, Kultida Woods did not tolerate ill-mannered behavior. She was the disciplinarian in the Woods household and she exercised it without hesitation. Kultida Woods came from a culture where a child's behavior reflected on the parent, and she would not allow her son to ruin her respectability. She also knew what was most important to her son. She later told John Strege, the author of *Tiger: A Biography of Tiger Woods*, "When I need to discipline Tiger, I take his golf clubs away. He stays in line pretty good that way." She explained to Tiger that golf was a gentleman's game, and it was intolerable to throw his clubs like a spoiled child who did not get his way. Both Earl and Kultida were supportive of Tiger's passion for golf and tried to do whatever they could to help him. Contrary to the stories that have sometimes circulated, however, they did not push their son to play. It was quite the opposite: Tiger had become hooked on the game long before his parents ever had to worry about the public's perception of them. They were not overbearing stage parents who lived through their son's success or viewed him as their ticket to wealth.

THE TIGER SETS HIS SIGHTS

The restrictions on where her son could play golf worried Kultida, so she began to look for other options. Her search turned up Heartwell Golf Park, a par-3 course located in Long Beach, about 10 miles (16 kilometers) from Cypress. Kultida met with Rudy Duran, an assistant pro at the park, and asked if

Rudy Duran (right) became Tiger's coach when Tiger was only four years old. At the time, Duran was an assistant pro at Heartwell Golf Park. When Kultida Woods requested permission for Tiger to play at the course, Duran was skeptical, but his doubts faded when he saw Tiger take a few shots.

Tiger would be allowed to play there. Duran wanted to see Tiger hit a few balls before he made a commitment. Once Tiger teed off on the driving range, Duran was not only convinced that the youngster could handle himself on the course, he was blown away by Tiger's poise, skill, and accuracy. Shortly after Tiger started to play at Heartwell, Duran became his first coach.

Duran was consistently impressed with Tiger's grasp of the game, his choice of clubs based on the shots he wanted to make, and his ability to think through the path to complete a hole. Duran explained in Strege's book, "We did an exhibition at Chalk Mountain [in Atascadero, California]. I'm talking about hundreds of people there, and I'm asking him to hit a variety of shots and he can understand the words I say and the process required and then execute the shots." It even seemed that Tiger could detect flaws in other competitor's swings and putts. His own swing seemed far more refined and precise than the swings of some golfers on the pro tour. By the time Tiger was six, he could drive the ball down the fairway more than 126 yards (115 m), even though he weighed less than 50 pounds (22.7 kg). He was not intimidated by any challenge in front of him on the course. When he was only seven years old, Tiger played a two-hole exhibition with legendary champion golfer Sam Snead. Despite hitting out of a tough spot near the water, Tiger lost to Snead by a mere one stroke. The story goes that after the exhibition, Snead offered Tiger his auto-graph. Tiger accepted it, but also offered Snead *his* autograph. Perhaps he already had expectations of where he would stand among golfer pros in the future.

Tiger's passion for golf would only deepen as he got older. He was becoming an exceptional player for his age, and he worked on his mental game almost as rigorously as his physi-cal game. Earl gave Tiger tapes to listen to with subliminal messages to help him master self-control and better mental discipline. Tiger himself wrote notes with motivational quotes and taped them to the walls in his bedroom. The one thing Tiger did not need was motivation to be the best. When he was still a preteen, Tiger made a three-column chart. In the first column he listed all the major golf tournaments. In the next column he wrote in Jack Nicklaus's age the first time he won a major championship. Finally, Tiger wrote his name at the top of the chart above the third column. His goal was to be the youngest player to win the majors like the Masters, the British Open, and the PGA Tour. Tiger told *Sports Illustrated* writer Tim Crothers, "Nicklaus was my hero, and I thought it would be great to accomplish all the things he did even earlier than he accomplished them." Who could have known that 11-year-old Eldrick "Tiger" Woods would indeed find himself in the company of such golf legends a few years later?

4

Training a Tiger

Tiger made his first birdie (finishing a hole one shot less than par, the number of strokes that a golfer should require to complete a hole) on August 27, 1980, which was quite a feat, even for a gifted child. He was just five years old and stroked the ball 91 yards (83 meters) in two shots into the cup on the third hole on the Heartwell Course. He recorded his first hole-in-one at age six on May 12, 1982. It was only a matter of time before Tiger would win his first sanctioned golf championship at the tender age of eight, capturing the first of his four Optimist International Junior World Championships (1982, 1983, 1987, and 1988). By 1987, Tiger would dominate the junior ranks of golf competitions in southern California, winning 30 junior tournaments.

MENTAL TOUGHNESS TRAINING

While in diapers, Tiger showed that he understood the rudimentary actions of playing golf: swing something at the ball,

The Game of Golf

The game of golf has many aspects, but it is not complicated. Brain Bank, an award-winning Web site, defines the game this way:

> Golf is an outdoor game in which players hit a small hard ball with specially designed clubs that consist of a metal shaft and a wooden or a metal club head. The object is to strike the ball with the club so that the ball goes into a cup that is sunk in the ground and marked with a flag. A standard golf course is divided into 18 holes, each with a tee, where the initial stroke is made; a grass fairway; and a green, a smooth grass surface where the cup is located.
>
> Each player attempts to reach the green and hit the ball into the cup using as few strokes as possible. Obstacles—such as water, tall grass called rough, or traps filled with sand—may be found near the green or fairway. As many as 14 different types of clubs may be used depending on the length of shot required or the terrain. The distance from tee to cup varies greatly, but generally it is from 100 to 600 yards [91 to 549 meters]. The length and difficulty of the hole determine the par, the number of strokes that a good golfer would need to put the ball into the cup. After 18 holes, the player with the lowest number of strokes is the winner of that round.*

Scoring terms identify how a golfer fared on a particular hole or what different parts of the golf course are called. For example, an *Eagle* means the golfer got the ball in the cup at a hole in two shots less than the number of strokes designated to complete the hole. A *bogey* on the other hand means that it took the golfer one more stroke that the number designed to complete the hole. A par-three hole is one in which it should take no more than three shots to get the ball into the cup. The *fairway* refers to the grassy area between the tee (where the first shot of the hole is taken) and the green. Some fairways can be as long as 600 yards (549 meters) or more, or as short as 100 yards (91 meters). The *green* is the target area, where the cup and the flag marking the hole are located. To make the game more challenging, hazards (water, tall grass, sand traps) are incorporated in the course design. Different clubs (woods, irons) weigh more than others and provide different power or effectiveness (sand wedge, putter) on the golf ball, and a good golfer needs to know which club selection is best suited for a particular shot and circumstance.

* Brain Bank, http://www.cftech.com/BrainBank/OTHERREFERENCE/SPORTSANDGAMES/Golf.html.

chase the ball, and hit it again. At an early age, however, he also demonstrated a keen understanding of the game's nuances. One day, while under the guidance of Rudy Duran, Tiger told his coach that he wanted to use a one-iron, which is the most difficult club to use. Duran cautioned Tiger that he would not be able to muster enough speed to get the club head on the ball to lift it in the air. Duran thought that was the end of it, until he saw Tiger on the driving range later that day. He was teeing off with his father's one-iron. Despite the fact that he was not much taller than the club, his strokes connected with the ball as well as they did with his regular club.

Earl Woods was pleased with his son's athletic progress on the golf course. It was only a matter of time before his son would beat him at the game they both loved. It took Tiger eight years to do so, but Woods felt that it was one competition he was willing to lose. He knew it was time to bring in a golf coach that could help his son reach the next level, and he found his man in John Anselmo. A former golfer on the PGA tour in the 1940s and 1950s, Anselmo was the head teaching coach at Los Altimos Golf Course in Cypress, California. He began to work with Tiger in 1986 to refine his swing and improve his visual imagery techniques. Anselmo worked with Tiger until he went off to college.

As Tiger's golf skills evolved rapidly, Woods shifted his attention in another direction. He knew his son would need to develop mental toughness to compete in the predominantly white man's sport. Most golfers and sports psychologists agree that the game of golf is 99 percent mental and 1 percent execution. Coach Jim Flick makes the point in his book, *Jim Flick on Golf*: "The game of golf begins in your mind, more than athletic ability, more than technique, more than practice or equipment or anything else. The mind-set or attitude you bring to the game determines not only the enjoyment you desire from golf but also the level of proficiency you will achieve." Flick was referring to a mental state that many people call being "in

Tiger Woods (right) and his caddie Jerry Chang share a laugh on the Magnolia Course at Walt Disney World Resort during a round of the National Car Rental Classic. Chang was a good friend of Tiger's when the two were in high school.

the zone." It is the ability to be completely engaged in an activity, feel a heightened focus, and attain success in the activity. It is similar to being so drawn into a book that the reader is not aware of noises, time of day, or other distractions. Instead, the reader experiences the sights, sounds, and smells described in the book.

As a former Green Beret, Earl Woods knew all about the psychological pressure tactics used in the military to maintain mental toughness during interrogations. He understood what it meant to be "in the zone." Woods wanted his son to be strong enough mentally to handle anything that came his way, whether it was a 60-foot (18-meter) putt on the golf course or a personal crisis. To do this, when he and Tiger played a round of golf, Woods would create every kind of possible distraction.

During golf tournaments, crowd roars can be heard several holes away from where the action has taken place. People cough and sneeze, camera motor drives whirl, clubs rattle in bags. To teach Tiger to focus completely on the moment, Woods might cough as soon as Tiger would start his swing or roll a ball in front of him just as he was ready to hit a putt. He used many tricks—whistling, shaking his car keys in his pocket, pulling the Velcro on his golf glove, dropping his golf bag, even telling Tiger that he better not hit the ball into the water—anything to break his concentration.

Sometimes during this toughness training, Tiger would stop in the middle of his swing and glare at his father. Woods just stood his ground and nonchalantly asked him why he was waiting. All this training paid off, although Tiger felt that it was one of the most difficult lessons in his young life. Earl Woods was the first to admit just how tough he had been. In *Tiger Woods: A Biography*, author Bill Guttman quotes Earl Woods:

> I taught him every trick an opponent could possibly pull, and some I invented myself. I'm not really proud of this, but I even cheated, just to get a reaction from him. Let's face it. Somewhere down the line somebody was going to do that, too. I made sure he was exposed to every devious, diabolical, insidious trick. It was a very difficult thing for me to do, and it didn't really fill me with pride and joy. But if he was going to continue in golf, I felt it was necessary.

Some might have questioned the seemingly harsh tactics that Woods used, but it only deepened the love and the trust between father and son. They had devised a code word for Tiger to use if the distractions were too much. If his son uttered the word, Woods would stop. According to Woods, Tiger never invoked the code word. To his father's credit, Tiger's mental toughness on the course impressed his coaches, the other players, and even fans watching from the time he started to compete. When asked later about his mental toughness, Tiger simply said he was the toughest golfer mentally, period.

INNER BALANCE

When asked about his wife during an interview with Clete Hux for the *Watchman Fellowship* article, "Towards an Understanding of New Age in Sports," Earl Woods made note that "Tida was meant to bring in the influence of the Orient, to introduce Tiger to Buddhism and inner peace, so he would have the best of two different worlds." Tiger was fortunate to have two parents who complemented each other. While Earl Woods was competitive and intense, Kultida Woods was quiet and had a calm demeanor. Much of that had to do with her Thai heritage. Kultida Woods was a Buddhist, and her faith emphasized an acceptance of the best and worst that happens in life, while sustaining an inner peace to keep life in balance, in harmony with one's surroundings. Buddhists teach that it is important to live a life with respect for others and maintain strong self-discipline. Tiger understood that Buddhism was a way of life very different from other religions and found contentment in his Asian heritage. He explains his feelings about Buddhism in *Tiger Woods: A Biography*:

> I like Buddhism because it's a whole way of being and living. It's based on discipline and respect and personal responsibility. I like the Asian culture better than ours because of that. Asians are much more disciplined than we are. Look at how well behaved their children are. It's how my mother raised me. You can question, but talk back? Never. In Thailand, once you've earned people's respect, you have it for life.

To introduce Tiger to his heritage, Kultida Woods took her son to Thailand when he was a preteen. Following a Thai custom, Kultida kept an astrological chart on Tiger from the time of his birth. While they were in the Thai capital city of Bangkok, Kultida visited with a Buddhist monk and gave him Tiger's chart to decipher. The monk told her that her son was special, that he had wondrous powers, and that he was going to be a leader someday. Kultida already knew this about her son. In "Towards an Understanding of New Age of Sports," Hux quoted Kultida: "Tiger has Thai, African, Chinese, American Indian and European blood. He can hold everyone together. He is the Universal Child."

To continue to provide the best foundation for their son to mature in the competitive world that athletes face, Earl and Kultida Woods enlisted the assistance of Jay Brunza, a sports psychologist. Brunza taught Tiger self-hypnosis and a few other techniques to keep him focused and relaxed, both on and off the golf course. It is very important not to lose one's cool during the pressure-induced moments when whether you win or lose depends on whether you make a great putt or can salvage a hole after you make a bad shot. Tiger used Brunza's techniques to think beyond the bad shot; he learned not to dwell or get flustered, but to look ahead and never look back. With these mental tools and his natural athletic talent, Tiger just needed to grow in size and weight to take his game to the next level.

TEEN PHENOMENON

In many ways, Tiger Woods was just like any other teenager in America. He ate pizza, went to the movies, rode his bicycle, and got his driver's license. He played video games, listened to music, and spent time with his two close buddies, Byron Bell and Jerry Chang. For most of Tiger's young life, he quarreled very little with his parents. When he became a teenager, Tiger and Earl Woods finally had something to disagree about: music. Earl was a fan of jazz. Tiger loved rhythm and blues (R&B) and rap. In a November 2001 *Golf Digest* article, Earl Woods had this to say, "We went through a point where Tiger

Jack Nicklaus, known as the "Golden Bear," drives a shot in 1978. At a young age, Tiger Woods was determined to match or beat the records of Nicklaus, whom he idolized.

had rap music that almost got him kicked out of the house. Neither my wife nor I understand rap. I don't consider it music. I don't hear anybody singing. It's just talking, and I don't understand the pronunciation. But far be it from me to judge. Just don't play it in my car."

Although Tiger may have behaved like any other teenager in many respects, he was anything but ordinary. His love of golf eclipsed involvement in any other sport. All through his youth, Tiger kept track of every milestone Jack Nicklaus achieved so that he could match or even exceed it. This was how Tiger set goals for himself and gauged his own progress. He knew that Nicklaus had broken a score of 50 on the front nine holes in 1950, when he was nine years old. Tiger had done that when he was three. Nicklaus first broke a score of 80 when he was 12; Tiger was 8 when he did the same. At 13, Nicklaus broke a 70 for the first time, but Tiger had achieved that milestone at age 12. True to his mental training, Tiger also looked ahead. He knew other achievements Nicklaus had reached before he turned professional, and he set his sights on them as well— Nicklaus won the Ohio State Junior Championship five times (first at age 12 and last at age 16), his first U.S. Amateur victory when he was 19, and his first professional major championship at the age of 22.

When Tiger turned 13, Earl Woods retired from his job at McDonnell Douglas in order to travel with his son to tournaments around the country. The summer before Tiger was to begin eighth grade at Orangeview Junior High, he played in his first national tournament, known as the Big I. The Insurance Youth Golf Classic, hosted by the Texarkana Country Club in Arkansas, was a big draw for amateurs because they would have a chance to be paired up with and compete against players on the professional tour. During the tournament, Tiger, then 5 foot 6 inches (168 centimeters) tall and weighing 107 pounds (48.5 kilograms), found out just how good he was when he beat eight of the pros. He was then paired up with John Daly, the two-time Arkansas Player of the Year and future PGA Champion. At one point, Tiger actually led by four strokes, and it took Daly's best game to beat the 13-year-old by two strokes. Tiger finished the tournament in second place overall behind Justin Leonard, a future multiple PGA Tour champion, and ahead of another future golf champion, David Duval. Tiger returned to the Big I tournament the following year and won, which made him the youngest player ever to take the trophy. He was only a freshman in high school. He came in second place at the PGA National Junior Championship and third at the U.S. Junior National Championship. To cap a great year, at just 14 years old, Tiger was named the 1990 Southern California Player of the Year. He would earn that honor again in 1991, 1992, and 1993.

In 1991, Tiger had his best year to date, winning eight tournaments including the U.S. Junior Championship (youngest ever to win the event), his sixth Optimist International Junior World title, and the Southern California Junior Championship. Not only was he the youngest to win the U.S. Junior Championship, he was also only the third black golfer to win a U.S. Golf Association (USGA) title. He was named American Junior Golf Association Player of the Year, Golf Digest Player of the Year (1991, 1992), Titleist-Golfweek National Amateur of the Year, and First Team Rolex Junior All-American (1991, 1992, 1993). It had been one of Tiger's goals to win the U.S. Junior Championship since he first became aware of tournaments and titles. Because it was the most important title to win in the junior ranks, the fact that Tiger was the youngest ever to achieve that victory was an added accomplishment for the teenager. This victory qualified Tiger for the U.S. Amateur Championship, and although he did not play very well, it gave him a new goal to attain.

In 1992, Tiger won five tournaments, and the most important was the U.S. Junior Championship. He again made it to the U.S. Amateur tournament, finishing in the top 32. Tiger was not used to finishing so far behind other golfers and was determined to capture the title that so far had eluded him. Nevertheless, Tiger was making his own records for the golf history books. No other golfer had ever won two Junior Championships two years in a row. Better still, before his amateur career was over, Tiger would claim a third U.S. Junior Championship, the only golfer to do so in three consecutive years.

Despite his meteoric rise, Tiger had his setbacks too. There was no question that he would play on the Pioneers, the golf team at his school, Western High. His presence was a real asset during tournament play. He was still just a teenager, though, whose game was not always perfect. In his sophomore year, the team made it to the league championship, playing against Valencia High. The Pioneers were on the verge of winning after Tiger's ball landed on the green at the eighteenth hole. He only needed to sink the ball in two shots, but he missed the cup both times. Disappointed, Tiger had a lapse in concentration, hurriedly tapping the ball past the cup in what would have been an easy three-putt and a tie. Instead, the Pioneers lost the championship. Tiger realized that he let his emotions get the better of him, but it was a good lesson to learn. He knew there was no room for careless errors in golf, and no place for a lapse in mental toughness. True champions never let up on a hole, a shot, or a putt. He just needed a gentle reminder to stay "in the zone."

5

The Future Cardinal Takes Flight

It was not easy for Tiger Woods to juggle schoolwork, a social life, and all the traveling that tournament play required. In addition to these commitments was the increased pressure to succeed, pressure and expectations that did not come from within himself or from his father. Although Tiger was a blend of so many ethnicities, he looked black and was perceived that way. As his successes on the links (another term for a golf course) grew, so did Tiger's fame. The young golfer's success generated chatter that he would become the great black hope in the sport. Tiger never minded being mentioned in the same conversation with Lee Elder, Charlie Sifford, Calvin Peete, or other black golf pros, but he did not want to be the best black golfer on the tour. He wanted to be known as the best golfer on the tour, period.

Tiger accepted invitations to play golf with pros like Greg Norman and Mark O'Meara. He also received a sponsor's invitation to play in the 1992 Nissan Los Angeles Open. Tiger dreamed about making his debut at the famed Riviera Country Club. The club had hosted a U.S. Open and a PGA Championship. It was near his home, and it was the place where celebrities played a round of golf for relaxation. The L.A. Open also gave Tiger an opportunity to play the game on a course with the galleries filled with spectators. He had never played in front of such a large crowd, and the experience was both exciting and humbling. Many curious people came out to see the 16-year-old that everybody in golf was talking about, and to get a glimpse of his game skills. On the first day, on the very first hole, Tiger made a birdie. He ended the day only one shot over par, but he was not happy with that score. Unfortunately, the next day he played even worse and did not make the cut to the round. Humble in his assessment of his play, he was quoted in John Strege's book *Tiger* as saying, "I learned that I'm not that good. I'm very disappointed I didn't make the cut. But give me some time to grow up and I'll be back. It's still the two best days of my life."

NEEDING MORE

Once Tiger had intermittent opportunities to play beyond the junior ranks, he wanted to increase the competition he faced. He was already ranked the number one junior player in the country and had won more trophies and medals than his family's small house in Cypress, California could hold. He accepted more invitations to play in some pro tournaments, including the Byron Nelson Classic, the Honda Classic, and another trip to the Los Angeles Open. Tiger again missed the cut in these tournaments, but he was gaining invaluable experience, as well as admiration from more and more pros. They were simply amazed at the skill set, poise, and demeanor of such a young talent. Nelson called pro champion Tom Watson and told him Tiger seemed to have no weaknesses in his game. Billy Andrade, a two-time winner on the PGA Tour said of Tiger in Guttman's

Tiger Woods, age 16, is shown in action in the Pro-Am portion of the Los Angeles Open at the Riviera Country Club on February 27, 1992. As a tenth grader, Tiger was the youngest player ever to compete in a PGA tour event when he participated in the tournament.

book *Tiger Woods: The Making of a Champion*, "Just looking at his swing, the length he hits the ball and the way he carries himself, he's just way ahead of any junior golfer I've ever seen."

It was a challenge for Tiger to be 17 years old and playing years beyond his physical age. At times he was exhausted by the travel pace, school, and just being himself. His celebrity status grew by the day, and more and more people seemed to want a piece of him in the form of autographs and interviews. Colleges actively recruited him, and it seemed that even pro management representatives were keeping an eye on him. Although people speculated that Tiger might skip college altogether and turn pro after he graduated from high school, such talk never happened in the Woods house. Tiger had already decided that he wanted to major in business, so he could keep better track of his earnings once he started to win the big money from pro events. Phil Mickelson, a multiple PGA Tour champion and winner of the U.S. Amateur Championship, was among many who counseled Tiger to have fun with golf at this stage in his life. In *Making of a Champion,* Mickelson said, "He's got a fun process ahead of him. The next four or five years, he's going to have a lot of fun playing in amateur events and collegiate golf. That would be what I would tell him—have fun."

One of the ways Tiger found to escape the pressure of the game, as well as the increasing expectations, was to conduct golf clinics for kids with his dad. Tiger was able to connect with the kids, perhaps because in many ways he was still just a kid himself. The clinics also taught Tiger an important lesson. *Tiger* author Strege wrote,

> On their travels, the pair conducted these clinics frequently, Earl's way of impressing on Tiger the importance of giving back to a game that had been generous to him. The message Earl was instilling in Tiger was that he has a responsibility to those who preceded him and to those who will succeed him. He not only must carry the torch of the past; he must further a cause that seems to have chosen him.

Tiger felt a particular responsibility to introduce what had primarily been an exclusive sport for mostly white males to kids in the inner city communities who might not otherwise have the opportunity to learn about and play golf.

For the teen who was looking for more, working with the kids in the clinics provided one such outlet. In *Tiger: A Biography of Tiger Woods*, Guttman quotes him saying, "I love doing clinics. I love helping them out. I think that's the biggest impact I've made so far. It doesn't matter whether they're white, black, brown, or green. All that matters is I touch kids the way I can through these clinics and that they benefit from them." He lived by the words he often heard from his parents: "care and share." The clinics became so popular that Tiger and his father were able to conduct them in places that would normally not be able to attract such programs. They put on a clinic in East Los Angeles, the rough and crime-riddled section of the city often in the news for its gang-related clashes and violence. Not only did rival gang members of the Crips and Bloods show up, they agreed not to wear their gang colors and not to engage in any hostilities during the clinic. Long before he became the icon of golf, Tiger was receiving the respect of a champion, and he found that the love and enjoyment he got from golf could affect the lives of others.

DECISION TIME

Tiger's junior year at Western High was full of achievements, but he also had a few disappointments. Scholastically, he was among the top students in his class, and he continued to rack up record after record, win after win, and award after award in golf. Among his latest honors was winning the Dial Award, presented to the top national high school male and female athletes in the country. He was named first team Rolex Junior All-American, and by winning his third-straight Junior Amateur title, he qualified once again for the U.S. Amateur tournament. It was the one title that had eluded Tiger. If he wanted to eclipse Jack Nicklaus in yet another achievement, he knew it would have to be soon because Nicklaus won the championship when he was 19, and Tiger was already 17. Unfortunately, 1993 was not to be the year. Tiger missed the cut at the end of the second round, but before he headed back to Cypress, he was introduced to Butch Harmon, known as one of the top golf instructors in the sport. His students have included top pros Greg Norman, Davis Love III, Fred Couples, and Justin Leonard. After he watched Tiger swing his club, Harmon felt that he could help take Tiger's game to the highest level, but it would take about three years before Tiger would be a fully developed golfer.

A great deal of Tiger's energies had been devoted to golf, but it was also time to make a decision about life after high school. Colleges and universities all over the country were vying for his commitment to attend their school. In Tiger's mind, there were really only three universities in the running: Stanford University, the University of Nevada at Las Vegas (UNLV), and Arizona State. All three schools are members of the National Collegiate Athletic Association (NCAA). Stanford had an edge because of its academic reputation. In addition, when Tiger was 13, he received a letter from the Stanford men's golf coach, Wally Goodwin. Goodwin had been following the teen's career and decided it was not too early to make Tiger aware that Stanford wanted him to attend the university and join the men's golf team. In his letter to Tiger, Goodwin wrote, "If you ever want to take a shot at Stanford, drop me a line." To Goodwin's amazement, Tiger wrote back to the coach to thank him for

IN HIS OWN WORDS...

"One of the things that my parents have taught me is never to listen to other people's expectations. You should live your own life and live up to your own expectations, and those are the only things I really care about."

his letter and tell him about his interests and future plans. The letter was written perfectly, with punctuation, spelling, and grammar on the level of someone much older.

Jack Nicklaus

One of the most successful professional golfers ever, Jack Nicklaus won an astonishing 113 professional tournaments, including 73 PGA tours, 10 senior PGA tours, and 30 unofficial and international events. In a career that spanned five decades, his name became synonymous with golfing greatness and changed the face of the sport itself.

Jack William Nicklaus was born on January 21, 1940, in Columbus, Ohio, to drugstore owner Louis Nicklaus and his wife, Helen. In 1950, at age 10, he began taking golf lessons at the Scioto Country Club with pro Jack Grout in 1950, by 1953 he'd won the Ohio State Junior Championship for boys ages 13–15 and the Columbus Junior Play Championship. He later captured two more titles, defeating the state's top pro and amateur in the 1956 Ohio Open.

Nicklaus earned a spot in the U.S. Open in 1957. In 1962, he turned pro. Labeled the "Golden Bear" by other golfers because of his blonde hair and large frame, he experienced his first professional victory, over heavily favored veteran Arnold Palmer, at the U.S. Open in Oakmont. By the end of the year, Nicklaus had racked up two more wins, the Seattle Open and the Portland Open, and was named Rookie of the Year.

Between 1962 and 1966, Nicklaus won 21 PGA events, including the Masters in 1965 and 1966. In 1966, Nicklaus also won the British Open at Muirfield in Scotland, becoming the youngest player (at age 26) to do so. This win also made him the only golfer after Gene Sarazen, Ben Hogan, and Gary Player (until Tiger Woods) to win all four major championships—a feat known as the "career slam." Before Tiger Woods, no golfer other than Jack Nicklaus had ever won every major tournament more than once.

After his U.S. Open victory in 1967, however, Nicklaus entered a slump from which he would not emerge until 1970. During these years, his physical condition declined and he gained weight. In 1970, Nicklaus's father, Charlie, died. Jack had already begun getting back in top shape, but his father's death was galvanizing. "My father passed away and I sort of realized that he had certainly lived his life through my golf game. I really hadn't probably given him the best of that. So I . . . got myself back to work."

With his victory at the 1971 PGA Championship, Nicklaus became the first golfer to win all four majors twice in a career. By year's end, he'd taken four

Tiger visited all three schools before he made his decision. The most important thing was which would offer Tiger the best education. He knew that his golf game would not improve

more tournaments, including the Tournament of Champions and the National Team Championship. In 1973, he not only picked up six more major tournament victories, but he was also named PGA Player of the Year for the third time. In 1974, he was one of the 13 original inductees into the World Golf Hall of Fame.

Nicklaus accomplished a triple career slam in 1978, winning all four majors for the third time—the only pro golfer ever to have done so. *Sports Illustrated* magazine named him Sportsman of the Year. But the grand victories preceded another career slump, during which he would not win another tournament until 1980. He rebounded with victories in the U.S. Open and the PGA Championship in 1980, but over the following five years he won only twice on the tour.

In 1986, Nicklaus became the oldest Masters winner in history, a record that still stands. Lacerated by one journalist for being "washed up," Nicklaus later said that the put-down was in part what spurred him to win. "I kept thinking all week, 'Through, washed up, huh?' I sizzled for a while. But then I said to myself, 'I'm not going to quit now, playing the way I'm playing. I've played too well, too long to let a shorter period of bad golf be my last.'"

In 1990, 50-year-old Nicklaus joined the senior tour circuit. He earned four Champions Tour victories, breaking the previous record by two. Nicklaus's one hundredth career win came in 1996, with his fourth victory at the Tradition—the last official win of his career.

Today, Nicklaus devotes much of his time to golf course design. With his four sons and one son-in-law, he operates Nicklaus Design, one of the largest golf design practices in the world. Nicklaus has also written a host of golf instruction books, including the classic *Golf My Way*, as well as an autobiography titled *My Story* and a volume on his golf course design methods and philosophy.

Nicklaus's career spanned five decades and included 105 professional tournament wins, a record 20 major championship titles, and the distinction of being the only player in history to have won each of golf's major tournaments at least twice.

tremendously at Stanford because of the academic demands, but in the end Tiger felt that Stanford was the best choice for him. He was going to be a Stanford Cardinal, the nickname of the athletic teams at the university. He made it official on November 10, 1993, in the gymnasium at Western High. Tiger would begin his collegiate career on a full scholarship in the fall of 1994. As he had always planned, Tiger chose the business program, where he could major in accounting. With more than six months left in his senior year, Tiger already had several high school and amateur tournaments scheduled to play before graduation, along with several events through the summer. Included in the list were professional events like the Buick Classic in New York.

PREPPING FOR THE BIG ONE

Tiger played out most of his tournaments unremarkably. The professional tournaments continued to be a great experience for the 17-year-old, even though he finished well behind pros like Greg Norman, Fred Couples, and Ernie Els. All in all, Tiger had a pretty good year. He was named *Los Angeles Times* Player of the Year, Orange County Player of the Year, and Orange County League Most Valuable Player (fourth time).

Despite all of the travel and demands of finishing high school, Tiger remained on an even keel and kept his priorities in order. He did not play in the U.S. Open Qualifying tournament because it fell on the same day as his graduation from Western High. There would be plenty of other U.S. Opens ahead, but he would only graduate from high school once.

After Tiger graduated with honors—which made his parents especially proud because they had always emphasized the importance of education—he played in several events over the summer, leading up to the U.S. Amateur tournament. He won the Western Amateur Championship, the Southern California Golf Association Amateur Championship (Southern Cal State Am), and led the U.S. Team at the World Amateur Team Championships in Versailles, France, to an 11-stroke victory. Tiger's performance at the Southern Cal State Am was one for the record books. He shot a course-breaking record and career-low 62 in the second round. Despite this, it was all about the U.S. Amateur Championship. If he won, Tiger would become not only the youngest player to do so, but the first person of color, as well.

TRIUMPH AT SAWGRASS

When Tiger first learned about golf tournaments and records and championships, he established a set of goals for himself based on the phenomenal achievements of Jack Nicklaus, and one by one, he accomplished them. All that was left for him now as an amateur was an NCAA title, which would rank him the number-one player in the country, and the U.S. Amateur Championship. On the hot and humid day of August 26, 1994, in Ponte Vedra, Florida, he walked on the course at the Tournament Players Club at Sawgrass Stadium, poised to make history. The U.S. Amateur Championship tournament is slightly different from other events in that all participants start off by playing two rounds of medal play (another term for stroke play, where the score is based on counting strokes), which is 36 holes of golf. Once those two rounds are completed, the 64 players with the lowest scores move on to match play, in which players go up against each other one-on-one, instead of one against the field as in stroke play. Contenders compete to win individual holes, and the player who wins the most holes wins the match. In match play, each match is 18 holes, with the winner advancing and the loser eliminated. The two remaining competitors play another 36 holes of match play. The finalist who wins the most holes earns the title of U.S. Amateur Champion.

With an ease he had demonstrated in so many tournaments over his amateur career, Tiger blew through the first two rounds of medal play, as he moved up with 63 other players onto match play. He made it through the round of 16, and he

Tiger Woods gives instructions to eight-year-old Damon Eames as part of a youth golf clinic at Fort Bragg's Stryker Golf Course. The clinic, part of the Tiger Woods Foundation, was organized for children whose parents are in the military. Woods decided to spend the week at Fort Bragg to try to better understand what his father, Earl, went through while he was stationed at Fort Bragg as a Green Beret.

beat back his first serious challenge from 1986 U.S. Amateur champion and University of Florida golf coach, Buddy Alexander in the round of 32. Tiger made it to the final, where he would play against Oklahoma State collegiate star Trip Kuehne, but things did not start well for Tiger. He found himself down 6 holes through 13 holes. No one had ever come back to win the U.S. Amateur after being so far down. At the end of the first 18 holes played, Kuehne had put up impressive stats: He posted a score of 66, with 7 birdies over the first 13 holes. Kuehne was up by four shots as the play ended for a lunch break.

Tiger should have felt that this latest chance to claim the elusive Amateur title was slipping away, but he knew his game was much stronger over a 36-hole game than an 18-hole game. Before Tiger stepped onto the first tee to start the next round of 18, Earl Woods pulled him aside to offer a pep talk: "Let the legend grow." Kuehne made a birdie on the second hole to go up again by five, but that would be his last birdie, and he would only win one more hole the rest of the way out. On the other hand, Tiger played historic golf, winning the fourth, seventh, ninth, tenth, eleventh, sixteenth, and seventeenth holes, some of them in dramatic fashion. On the seventeenth hole, for example, Tiger made a 14-foot (4.25-meter) putt after toying with the precarious par-three hole surrounded by water, always a hazard for a golfer. When he sank the putt to go up by one with one hole to play, Tiger pumped his fist into the air in celebration. Keuhne's father, observing the play, could only watch in awe, later saying that putt had "divine intervention," something people had been noticing about the phenomenal player from Cypress, California.

After what had happened on the seventeenth hole, the eighteenth paled in comparison. Kuehne must have been disheartened by the stunning turn of events, even missing a 6-foot (2-meter) putt for par. It was over in dramatic fashion. Tiger had won the U.S. Amateur Championship, in the most amazing comeback in the 99-year history of the tournament. He also became the youngest player to do so, again eclipsing a Nicklaus record. Tiger later said that the win did not sink in until he embraced his father, who was waiting to congratulate his son on the green. The match had been broadcast nationally on ESPN, and suddenly a floodgate of congratulations seemed to come from everywhere. Tiger received letters from pro golfer Gary Player and comedian Sinbad, as well as phone calls from Reverend Jesse Jackson and representatives from the *Tonight Show with Jay Leno* and the *David Letterman Show*, who wanted Tiger as a guest on their shows. Tiger shunned the publicity and turned down their requests. A letter from U.S. President Bill Clinton became a permanent part of the family wall; it read in part, "I commend you for the sportsmanship, discipline, and perseverance that earned you this great honor. Best wishes for every success at Stanford."

When Tiger returned home, the Cypress Country Club had an event to honor him. He was even given a key to the city. His face was splashed on the front page of the *New York Times* and *USA Today*. Talk and speculation followed about what Tiger would do next. He was not yet a Stanford freshman, he had not taken his place on the Stanford Cardinals golf team or even settled in to his dorm room, yet already there was a buzz in the golf world about how long Tiger would wait before turning pro. For the moment, Tiger just wanted to savor his latest accomplishment and plan out his schedule of classes for his first semester in college. He did not want to focus on the questions about turning pro, and he would not let them distract him from what was just beyond the California horizon.

6

When to Turn Pro?

Stanford University consistently ranks as one of the top universities in the country. It includes seven schools that offer undergraduate and graduate degrees in the humanities and sciences, engineering, earth sciences, business, law, education, and medicine. Among Stanford's many graduates are Nobel Prize laureates, Pulitzer Prize winners, and seven recipients of the Presidential Medal of Freedom. As the school states on its Web site, "The Stanford motto, 'The wind of freedom blows,' is an invitation to free and open inquiry in the pursuit of teaching and research. The freedom of scholarly inquiry granted to faculty and students at Stanford is our greatest privilege; using this privilege is our objective."

The academic and cultural diversity of Stanford's student body is immediately apparent. One class might have a rising classical pianist, a medical researcher who will find the cure for cancer, and a collegiate athlete who might win the Sullivan Award, which honors the outstanding athlete of the year in the United States. Stanford has been the chosen institution of future Supreme Court Justices, NASA astronauts, artists, musicians, politicians, writers, and athletes. Within this eclectic environment, Tiger Woods would get his college education.

Woods settled into college life, comfortable as just another Stanford student. There was no celebrity treatment, nothing out of the ordinary, unless you were looking from the outside in. In his dorm there was a kid who could split atoms and had scored 1580 (1600 was a perfect score) on his Scholastic Aptitude Test (SAT), a defensive lineman on the Stanford football team who scored 1500 on his SATs, and a guy who scored 1580 on his SATs and never needed to study because he had a photographic memory. For the first time, Woods was among some of America's brightest, all in one place. It was a welcome change. In *Tiger Woods: The Making of a Champion*, author Tim Rosaforte quotes Woods as he summed up his impressions of freshman life, saying, "Nobody sleeps here. There's so much work you have to stay up late. But it's easy to blend in here because everyone's so special. You have Olympian swimmers, baseball and football players who are going to be in the pros . . . and I'm not the brightest one, either. There are geniuses here."

LIFE AS A CARDINAL

On the university golf team, Woods found himself the newbie among 1993–1994 NCAA champions. All the members of the team were seniors, and there were promising future pros: Notah Begay, team captain and two-time All-American; Casey Martin, Oregon State Champion, 1994 All-American, 1995 All-American Scholar; Steve Burdick, 1994 All-American; and William Yanigisawa, 1994 All-American. As the only freshman on the team, Woods had to tote bags like any other freshman, and when on the road at competitions, three in a room meant

Tiger Woods (back row, fourth from left) and his Stanford University golf team, the Cardinals, pose for a team picture in 1994 at the Stanford University golf course.

Woods got the rollaway bed. The other guys often teased him, especially Begay. When Woods took out his contact lenses and put on his glasses, Begay called him "Urkel" after the nerdy Steve Urkel from the television show *Family Matters*. During one road trip early on, the guys played a practical joke on Woods, poking fun at his celebrity. Martin disguised his voice on a call to Woods's hotel room and pretended to be a news reporter. Martin asked Woods totally off-the-wall questions, which the freshman tried to answer as tactfully as he could. Finally the pranksters could not contain their laughter, and Woods knew it had been a joke. Some people would have been upset, but Woods took it in stride.

Woods wanted to take in as much of the college life experience as he could handle, so he joined the Sigma Chi fraternity and, like any other teenager, enjoyed the camaraderie, socializing, and parties that were part of fraternity life. Although he had plenty of coordination on the golf course, he was not as comfortable off the course. The first time he stepped onto the dance floor at one of his fraternity's parties, it became apparent that dancing was not one of his talents. Woods earned the nickname "Dynamite," because his moves reminded his friends of someone trying to detonate explosives.

Once Woods was back on a driving range or a golf course, though, he was no longer Dynamite; he was one of the best golfers Stanford had ever seen. His teammates marveled at his command and control of his clubs and the ball. In Strege's book *Tiger*, teammate Jake Poe related an encounter between himself and Woods:

> He was looking at me and I punched a 4-iron shot at him and got it rolling toward his feet. He's still walking and in mid-stride he grabs his driver with his other hand. He's got it in both hands now and the ball's rolling at a good pace, and in mid-stride, still walking, he takes a full swing and hits the ball at least 290 yards, a slap shot, perfectly straight. Probably the most impressive shot I've ever seen. Everything in full motion—him, the ball, everything. Incredible.

SWINGING HIS CLUBS IN BOTH WORLDS

Even before his first day at Stanford, Woods claimed victory at his first collegiate event and won the Tucker Invitational by three strokes. Although Woods may have had the mindset to win every tournament, he knew that was not possible. There were plenty of third, fourth, and even lower place finishes in his team play, but for Woods, it was all part of the process necessary to turn pro. Woods also won the Jerry Pate Invitational at Shoal Creek, in Birmingham, Alabama. It was the last tournament Woods would win in his freshman year, but it was an especially sweet victory for him because of the past racial discrimination practices by the Shoal Creek Country Club.

Because Woods had won the U.S. Amateur, he received an invitation to play in perhaps the most prestigious of all the PGA tournaments: the Masters in Augusta, Georgia. His appearance in the tournament was just a matter of time, as a college athlete or as a pro. It was one of the most anticipated moments in the sport since Tiger Woods began to carve out his own place in golf history. A black player had not participated in the Masters for 20 years, several months before Woods was even born. Now, on April 6, 1995, the 19-year-old would make his debut. As an amateur, Woods was excluded from any money winnings, but it was priceless just to have the experience of playing on the course with Greg Norman, Phil Mickelson, Tom Watson, his hero Jack Nicklaus, and 1995 winner Ben Crenshaw. Woods finished in forty-first place, three over for the tournament, coming in ahead of two pros, John Daly and Seve Ballesteros. Woods made history again as the only amateur player to make it through all four rounds.

Before he left Augusta National, Woods wrote a letter of appreciation to all those who had made his presence at the tournament possible. He read the note to the media: "Please accept my sincere thanks for providing me the opportunity to experience the most wonderful week of my life. It was Fantasyland and Disney World wrapped into one . . . I've accomplished much here and learned even more . . . It is here that I left my youth behind and became a man. For that I will be eternally in your debt."

At Augusta, many caught their first glimpse of this teen golf marvel, but it would not be their last. What they might not have known was that, despite the pressures of appearing in his first Masters, Woods had slipped off the grounds at Augusta National after the second round of the tournament. He met up with some of the black caddies at the club to conduct a golf clinic for a group of young black kids from the other end of town. Of the more than 900 golfers who have played in the Masters, Tiger Woods was the only one who had ever taken the time to give a clinic. The rest of the time he was there, Woods had to divide his time between his tournament responsibilities and a history exam that awaited his return to Stanford.

Before he began his sophomore year at Stanford, Woods won his second U.S. Amateur title, and surpassed another Nicklaus feat. Nicklaus had never won two Amateurs consecutively, and only eight other players had ever done so since the tournament began. The win also secured a return to the Masters, the U.S. Open, and the British Open the following year.

As Woods began to play in both the amateur and professional worlds, he had occasional worries in the back of his mind about the million dollar question: Would he complete his college education before he turned pro? Woods always returned to two things when he thought about his answer. Nicklaus and Phil Mickelson had been the only two golfers ever to win the NCAA championship and the U.S. Amateur title in the same year. No player had ever won three consecutive U.S. Amateur championships. There was still room for Woods to achieve as an amateur player. He also knew how important it was to get a good education. He wondered if his parents would be disappointed if he left Stanford before he graduated. His life in college was enjoyable, but he wanted to take his game to the next plateau in his life. Woods made his decision on the most important point. He knew his game was not yet ready to compete consistently and win tournaments on the professional level. Woods would be satisfied for now with his pursuit of the Golden Bear: Jack Nicklaus.

THE YEAR OF THE TIGER

Woods started the year with a second-place finish by the Cardinals at the February 1996 Ping Intercollegiate in Tucson, Arizona. Woods placed second in the individual scoring. Two weeks later, he won the John Burns Invitational in Kaneohe,

Hawaii. After a rather disappointing outing at the Golf Digest Collegiate in early March, Woods returned to winning form, and took the title at Southwestern Intercollegiate tournament in California. He only played one more tournament, and finished third at the U.S. Collegiate before he made his second trip to the Masters.

As Woods arrived at the Masters for his second appearance in the tournament, he seemed a bit drained from the rigorous pace and his ever-present schoolwork. If the truth were known, Woods was becoming a bit bored with college golf, and although he had moved from freshman gopher to the Cardinals' team leader, his academic work was becoming more difficult to get through. Woods was not one of the geniuses at Stanford, and he had to work hard to maintain decent grades. He was also becoming increasingly annoyed that the NCAA was citing him for so many infractions. One time it was for using Maxfli golf balls instead of the Titleist ones used by the Cardinals. Another time it was because the NCAA felt a little bit uncomfortable with the number of professional tournaments Woods had attended. The final straw was when Woods reported a lunch he had with Arnold Palmer the previous fall in which Palmer paid the bill, even though Woods had offered to pay for his own meal. The scrutiny was getting to Woods, and he felt that in some ways it was over the top. He had met with Palmer to discuss his future as a professional, and he looked to the elder statesman of the sport to offer insight on how to deal with all the celebrity attention. Ultimately, Woods wrote Palmer a check for the lunch, and he started to think more seriously of turning professional, perhaps sooner rather than later.

During the practice rounds, Woods got a charge out of walking onto the course with a legend on either side of him: Arnold Palmer and Jack Nicklaus. When it came time to play, however, Woods was uncharacteristically distracted by the barrage of questions from the media about when he was going to turn

Ray Floyd (left) and Greg Norman of Australia (center) watch as amateur Tiger Woods tees off during practice in Augusta, Georgia, in April 1994.

professional. His concentration was off and he missed the cut after the second round concluded. Woods, disappointed in his play and frustrated that he had not at least made the cut like he had the previous year, caught a flight back to Palo Alto, where he immediately had to write an economics paper. The rest of the year would have a remarkable upturn for Woods, and it would solidify his place in the amateur world of golf.

Woods won several more collegiate tournaments in his run up to the NCAA Championship, held from May 29 to June 1, 1996, including the Cougar Classic, the Pac-10 (Tiger shot a first round course 61), and the NCAA West Regional. There were just two things left to accomplish: The NCAA Championship title and a third U.S. Amateur title. Tiger's first test to make both a reality was the NCAA Championship at the Honors Course in Chattanooga, Tennessee. Woods started off in spectacular form, just one stroke behind Pat Perez of Arizona State after the first round. In the second round, Woods shot a course record-breaking 67, giving him a three-stroke lead with two rounds to go. After he increased his lead by two strokes in the third round, Woods stumbled a bit, shooting an 80 in the final round. Still, he finished four strokes ahead of Arizona's Rory Sabbatini, and he captured his first NCAA Championship. The tournament finished out Tiger's collegiate events for the year, and shortly after the tournament he flew to Dublin, Ohio, to receive the Jack Nicklaus Trophy, awarded to the top college player of the year. In a single day, Woods had matched his hero's record and was the recipient of the trophy that bore his name.

All that was left for Woods now was to win the U.S. Amateur. He played the U.S. Open, and although he actually led through 13 holes of the first round at the Oakland Hills Country Club in Birmingham, Michigan, his game seemed to fall apart and he finished tied for eighty-second place. He moved on to play at the British Open, where he fared much better and finished in a tie for twenty-second place. As a surprise bonus, Woods was presented with the Silver Medal, awarded to the amateur with the lowest (best) score. A poor performance in the Western Amateur in Benton Harbor, Michigan, where Woods was out after the first round, sent him off to spend some time to think about what lay ahead. Professional golfer Curtis Strange had been one of those who were more open in his opinion about Woods's readiness to turn pro. During the telecast of the British Open, Strange said, "I've thought he should turn pro the last three, four, five months. He's ready physically. He's mature enough. He has nothing else to prove whatsoever in amateur golf. The quicker he gets out here, the quicker he gets to be the best player in the world."

When Woods returned from Michigan, he sat down with his father and told him he had made a decision. He knew he was ready. He had always said he would know when the time came. Woods told his parents that he would defend his U.S. Amateur title and then announce his decision to turn pro when he played at the Greater Milwaukee Open the following week. Earl and Kultida Woods made their son promise them one thing before they would give him their blessing: At some point along the way, he would finish school. Woods promised, and the decision was finally made. The questions from the media and all the speculation were about to end. Woods was both relieved and excited about his decision. He had enjoyed his time at Stanford, but now it was time to look ahead.

7

High Expectations, Great Rewards

Life as Tiger Woods had known it for 20 years was about to change. Until he made his decision to leave school early, his life had been rather straightforward. As a youngster, his parents had taken care of all of his needs and had paid for whatever he needed for his golf career. They were the ones who made the financial and parental sacrifices so that Woods could play golf. The expectations placed on him were that he be a good person, try to do his best in all situations, and get a good education. He was a good son, who was always appreciative of his parents' help. In return for his parents' sacrifices, he did well in school, was a good kid who stayed out of trouble, was respectful and loving, and took his sport seriously so his parents' efforts were not wasted.

The situation was very similar when Woods went off to Stanford. His college expenses were covered by his scholarship, and his only responsibilities were to apply himself to his studies and make sure he was a Cardinal team player, who tried

Tiger Woods lines up a putt during the second day of qualifying rounds in the U.S. Amateur golf championship in North Plains, Oregon, on August 20, 1996. It would be Woods's last amateur tournament before he turned pro.

to play his best golf at all times. The people who surrounded Woods made life rather easy for him in a world that was anything but easy. Growing up in a working-class environment and playing an elitist's game certainly had its ironies.

All of that was going to change as soon as Woods stepped off the course at Pumpkin Ridge in Cornelius, Oregon, at the conclusion of the U.S. Amateur Championship. Win or lose, Woods was turning pro, and the world would never be the same again. He would no longer fly in coach class, stay in cheap motels when traveling, or strain the finances of his parents. Turning pro, no matter how much anxiety it initially produced, could be very lucrative for someone with Woods's talents.

As soon as his son announced that he was turning pro, Earl Woods began to work in the background to ensure his son's professional future. He began to negotiate with the International Management Group (IMG) early in summer 1996. IMG describes itself on its Web site as "the world's premier and most diversified sports, entertainment and media company. We partner with the world's leading marketers and media networks to help them grow their businesses through our event properties, media production and distribution, talent brands, sponsorship consulting, brand licensing, sponsorship sales and other services." Their first client was none other than Arnold Palmer.

Over time, IMG signed many other great sports personalities including Gary Player, Olympic skier Jean-Claude Killy, race car driver Jackie Stewart, tennis champion Andre Agassi, and Martina Navratilova. Earl and Tiger Woods thought IMG would be the best management agency to make the most of Tiger Woods's Asian identity, since they were a worldwide company. The plan was to maximize Woods's star marketability internationally, and spread his appeal to a worldwide audience. No contracts would be signed, however, until after Woods officially announced his intention to turn pro.

ENDINGS AND BEGINNINGS

While Woods prepared for his last U.S. Amateur Championship, IMG worked on his first lucrative endorsement deal: a five-year, $40 million deal with Nike. Press kits were ready to be mailed, along with a news release that announced that Woods would enter the pros.

Although only a select few knew of the plans, when Woods arrived at the Ghost Creek Course at Pumpkin Ridge to tee off on the first hole, he piqued the curiosity of some of those around him because he was no longer wearing the customary shorts of an amateur. Instead Woods showed up wearing long pants, perhaps a subtle tip-off to what people had been waiting to hear.

If ever Woods needed to find his "zone," the Amateur tournament was it. Even as he teed off, he had to find a way to quell all other thoughts. Some thoughts involved the past and the desire to eclipse another golf legend, Bobby Jones, with this win. Some thoughts involved the future. Before the tournament, Woods had begun to set up his own corporation, ETW, to help position himself for the sudden financial surge about to enter his life. He was closing on a townhouse in Orlando, Florida, to be his primary residence to avoid the huge California state tax. Even at 20 years of age, Woods understood how lucrative the Nike endorsement was, and what the company endorsement had done for Chicago Bulls star Michael Jordan. Almost overnight, the young college student and Cardinal team golfer, whose biggest decisions had been which club to use for which shot, suddenly had to make decisions about contracts, buying property, and looking for tax shelters for his impending wealth.

If his mental toughness had ever been in doubt, Woods's qualifying rounds of 69 and 67 put a rest to the questions. Once more, his score was the lowest after the first two rounds, which earned him the Amateur medal. In match play, Woods made a 40-foot (12-meter) putt on the eighth hole, which pretty much secured the win over Colorado senior J.D. Manning, 3 and 2. His next opponent was more troublesome. Jerry Courville was a 37-year-old amateur with plenty of experience. But Woods's trademark relentlessness finally overcame

Courville, and he won the match 4 and 2. Facing his first younger opponent, Charles Howell, Woods elevated his game, making it to the 553-yard (506-meter), par-5 eleventh hole in two strokes. Howell was just thankful that he played competitively, losing 3 and 1. Woods made it through the quarterfinal round and faced his Cardinal teammate Joel Kribel, the only four-time All-American at Stanford. In their semifinal match, Kribel was up 2 holes on Woods by the tenth hole, but Woods chipped away at the lead, with special help from an eagle on the fourteenth hole. As had all of his other opponents to that point, Kribel lost in a match 3 and 1, where Woods ran his streak to 26 holes without a single bogey.

DRAMATIC WIN, END OF SUSPENSE

Only one opponent stood between Woods and history. His name was Steve Scott, and he was a formidable challenger who was an All-American at the University of Florida. It was one of the most exciting finals in U.S. Amateur history. Woods's double-bogey on the second hole ended his no-bogey streak, and his two shots into the water at the par-3 fifth, gave Scott a three-hole lead. By the time the first 18 holes had been completed, Scott had a five-hole lead. Coach Butch Harmon noticed something off in Woods's swing and helped him make an adjustment during the break between rounds. Never one to panic, Woods slowly worked his way back and tied the match with a 30-foot (9-meter) putt on the seventeenth green.

The score remained the same through the eighteenth hole: Scott and Woods were headed to a playoff. At the first hole, Scott had a chance to win, but his birdie shot rolled just to the edge of the hole. The next hole ended the tournament when Woods's tee shot landed about 7 feet short of the hole, and Scott's tee shot landed beyond the green in some taller grass. Scott heroically tried to chip the ball as close to the pin as he could, but it stopped 6 feet away. On Woods's next play, he putted his ball to within 18 inches (46 centimeters) of the cup. Scott's putt just missed the cup, which left Woods to tap his shot in for the win and yet another write up in the history books. Even Hollywood could not have scripted a better ending to Woods's amateur career.

Nike sponsored a private party for the Woods family following the tournament. Although Woods was elated to be finished with his amateur stint, he was also exhausted. The following day, a Nike corporate jet flew Tiger and his parents to Milwaukee, Wisconsin, where Woods was to make his long-awaited announcement. All the frenzied activity over the last several days had taken a toll on the 20 year old. He was struggling under the enormous pressure to keep his pro plans secret until the formal announcement on Wednesday. As fate would have it, word somehow leaked to the media on Tuesday. Annoyed and relieved at the same time, Woods put an end to the leaks and speculation when he released the following statement, which read, in part: "This is to confirm that, as of now, I am a professional golfer. I will not answer any questions, or have any further comment, until tomorrow at 2:30 P.M. at my scheduled press conference."

While Woods was trying to focus on practicing for the Greater Milwaukee Open, IMG had signed another lucrative endorsement deal for their star client. Woods would agree to use Titleist's golf balls, golf gloves, and golf bags. For his endorsements, Titleist would pay Woods $3 million over three years. Although he had to borrow the $100 entry fee to play in the Open, Woods was now worth $43 million in endorsements alone. With the money he could earn on the pro tour, Woods could be one of the wealthiest men in golf before he reached his twenty-first birthday.

The press conference was anticlimactic. Seeming uncharacteristically nervous, Woods's first words as a pro were "Well, I guess, hello world." He then explained how he had reached his decision to turn pro and not return to Stanford to complete his last two years of college. After he answered as many questions from the press as he could, he excused himself to take care of some business matters, which included signing his multimillion-dollar contract with Nike. The next day, he played his first tournament as a pro. The news seemed to bring even larger crowds and greater media coverage than usual, but Woods just focused on his game. He shot a respectable 67—four under par in the first round—and made par the following day. Much to his dismay, when he looked up at the leader board, he saw that he was already eight shots back. He wondered what you had to do out on the course to be among the leaders.

"LEARNING FROM MY MISTAKES"

Exhaustion finally overtook Woods on the third day and he shot a 73, two over for the round. He finished the match tied for sixteenth place and earned $2,544. He fared better in his next tournament, where he finished eleventh at the Canadian Open and earned $37,500. At the Quad City Classic, Woods played so well through three rounds that he was in the lead by one. There was great anticipation that Woods was going to win in only his third tournament as a pro, but his game fell apart in the final round and he finished tied for fifth place. Woods continued to improve in his finishes, coming in third at the B.C. Open. His purse amounts grew, too. After four weeks on the tour, Woods had earned more than $140,000 dollars, which placed him just three positions below the top-125 money

IN HIS OWN WORDS...

"I had intended to stay in school, play four years at Stanford, and get my degree. But things change. I didn't know my game was going to progress to this point. It became harder to get motivated for college matches, and since I accomplished my goal of winning the NCAA, it was going to get harder still. Finally, winning the third Amateur in a row is a great way to go out. I always said I would know when it was time. Now is the time."

winners needed to get his PGA tour card. That was an important milestone because it would exempt Woods from having to qualify for tournaments the following year.

Woods's first misstep in golf etiquette took place in September at the Buick Challenge in Georgia. Not only did his presence create a lot of excitement, but he was also going to be honored at a dinner after completing the first round. Woods had been chosen as the 1996 recipient of the Fred Haskins Award, which is comparable to the Heisman Trophy for college football. Woods went out to play the first practice round on Tuesday with fellow pros Davis Love III, Peter Jacobson, and Jeff Sluman. After just nine holes, Woods called it a day. To everyone's surprise, on Wednesday morning he notified officials that he was withdrawing from the tournament due to fatigue. His decision created a negative backlash from the press and many of the pros. Perhaps withdrawing would have been acceptable as a college athlete, but it was not appropriate for a professional. As a result, the Haskins Award dinner was cancelled, and more than 200 people who had come to Pine Mountains to attend were disappointed. It was a public relations disaster for Woods.

Woods wrote a letter of apology to everyone who had planned to come to the dinner, as well as a piece for *Golf World* entitled "Learning from my Mistakes." He recognized that it was a mistake to withdraw and therefore disappoint the fans who were to attend the dinner. The only other thing Woods could do was get back to the tour and let his clubs speak for him. His next chance came in October at the Las Vegas

DID YOU KNOW?

Tiger always wears red on the final day of a tournament because his mother feels it is a powerful color.

According to Kultida Woods (left), red is a lucky color, so Tiger Woods always wears red clothing on his last day in a tournament. His biggest fans, his mother and his wife, Elin Nordegren, also wear red in support, as they do in this photograph from 2002.

Invitational. As his father had predicted, Woods won a PGA tournament before the end of the 1996 season. In just his fifth event as a pro, Woods had won his first tournament and the $297,000 winner's check.

Six more tournaments remained in the 1996 season. Woods won his second event on the PGA Tour by defeating former Open champion Payne Stewart by one stroke at the Disney World/Oldsmobile Classic in Lake Buena Vista, Florida. He had been sick the night before, but he learned from his mistake at Pine Mountain, and he played through it. In winning his second PGA tournament that year, Woods became only the second player (Robert Gamez won two in 1990) to do so in PGA history. The $216,000 winner's check ensured that Woods would finish in the top-125 moneymakers for 1996, which was a tremendous relief to him. He had also accomplished all that he had set out to do in 1996. He had won both the NCAA and U.S. Amateur championships and had played well enough after turning pro to earn a spot on the tour the following year. In fact, because he earned enough prize money to be in the top-30 money winners, he earned a two-year exemption and automatically qualified for the Tour Championship the following week in Tulsa, Oklahoma.

MORE IMPORTANT THINGS THAN GOLF

Woods's first round at the Southern Hill Country Club was unimpressive. What should have been a routine evening of rest for the second round the following morning turned into an anxiety-filled night at Saint Francis Hospital. At 2:00 A.M., Earl Woods awakened to chest pains, and his wife called the hotel desk to get him to the hospital. Earl Woods had been a chain smoker for decades, and had undergone quadruple bypass heart surgery 10 years earlier. Despite Kultida's suggestion that he stay at the hotel and sleep, Tiger spent the night with his parents, finally leaving in the early morning to grab a few hours of sleep before tournament play resumed. There was no way that Woods could find his "zone" on this day. His thoughts were entirely focused on his father; even after his mother arrived on the course later in the day to reassure Woods that his father was stable, he never found his groove. He finished the day eight over par, but considering where his concentration was, it could have been a lot worse. No one would have found fault if Woods had decided to withdraw from the Tour, but he knew that his father would not want him to. Still, Woods had said that night, "I didn't want to be here today because there are more important things in life than golf. I love my dad to death, and I wouldn't want to see anything happen to him."

Woods finished the tournament tied for twenty-first place. When his father was discharged from the hospital, Woods flew the family home on a chartered jet. His newfound wealth allowed him to be able to do things for his parents for a change. Woods had also matured greatly over the year; as part of this, he set out to right a wrong before the year was over. When Earl was well enough to travel again, he and Tiger set off on a rescheduled date to Pine Mountain, Georgia, where Tiger stood before those he had snubbed several weeks earlier. When he spoke, it was mostly to apologize, not to talk about the accomplishments that earned him the Fred Haskins Award. Earl Woods was proud of his son that night, not just for his athletic achievements, but also for his integrity.

At the J.C. Penney Classic in December, Woods came in second, ending an incredible, awe-inspiring year. He was named Sports Illustrated Sportsman of the Year, PGA Tour Rookie of the Year, and Jack Nicklaus Player of the Year. In addition, by the end of 1996, he ranked thirty-third in the world, the quickest rise into the top 50 in golf history. His sudden wealth was staggering. In just eight PGA Tour events as a pro, Woods had earned $790,594, placing twenty-fifth on the money list. If this is what he accomplished at age 20, what would he do at 21, 22, or 30?

8

A Life and Career in Balance

Woods's first full year on the pro tour, 1997, started with a sudden-death win over Tom Lehman at the Mercedes Championship in Hawaii. The match between Woods and Lehman was a classic battle, where each player made a great shot only to see his opponent "counter-punch" with his own great stroke.

Woods planned to play in 25 tournaments that year, including all four majors: the Masters, the U.S. Open, the British Open, and the PGA Championship. He had learned that he needed to pace himself so he would not tire like he had the year before. One major difference in his life was that he no longer had to juggle school, collegiate tournaments, and pro events.

At other tournaments early in the year, Woods was up and down. One week he finished eighteenth in the Phoenix Open, only to come back seven days later and just miss a win at the Pebble Beach Pro-Am. Woods was big news wherever he played; even on the days when it was apparent he was not going to win a tournament, the crowds went crazy when they caught a glimpse of his greatness on the course. Such a moment happened at the Phoenix Open when Woods hit a hole-in-one off the sixteenth tee. Nick Price, who was already in the clubhouse, heard a thunderous roar. He simply said, "Had to be an ace. Had to be Tiger."

Woods was in demand everywhere he went. People sought autographs, interviews, and appearances on television. Wherever he went, huge money followed in appearance fees. Even though fees were prohibited on the PGA Tour, there were other ways Woods was given incentives to accept an invitation to play. At the Phoenix Open, Woods conducted a golf clinic at the TCP course for 1,500 underprivileged youths. Some felt that this was a violation of the PGA Tour rules, but Tim Finchem, Tour commissioner, explained that everyone wanted Woods to play at their tournaments and assured everyone that Woods would do his best to spread his schedule around to play in as many events as he could. Celebrity had its difficulties.

In February, Woods flew to his mother's homeland to play in the Asian-Honda Classic in Bangkok, Thailand. When Woods landed during the night, he was greeted by hundreds of people who came out to welcome him. As Thai garlands covered his neck, Kultida Woods (who had flown out two weeks prior to her son's arrival) walked out to meet her son, accompanied by many family members. In the United States, Woods was considered a black American, but in Thailand, he was seen as pure

IN HIS OWN WORDS...

"I thought if I kept progressing in golf and I came on the Tour and did really well, I could help golf, bring more minorities into the game, and make it more diverse. I thought that would be my biggest impact. But the impact on the kids is something I love to do. I love doing clinics. I love helping them out."

Thai. The trip was important to Kultida, who wanted her son to experience her motherland.

Thailand also boasts more than one million golfers who play on 200 courses throughout the country, and many thought that Woods's appearance might help increase the number of golf enthusiasts and boost tourism to Thailand. Woods won the Asian-Honda Classic, finishing 20 under par. Although he had wanted to please his mother, Woods had no down time throughout the entire week. He recognized that big appearance fees (he reportedly was paid $300,000) had their own price. The international travel had sapped his energy and he was tired. Woods knew he had to be more careful about his schedule or he would burn out like he did before Pine Mountain.

THE FIRST GREEN JACKET

After finishing eighth in the Australian Masters, Woods and his mother flew back to the States. He played a few other

The Masters Tournament

By 1934, golf pros Bobby Jones and Clifford Roberts had already built a successful golf course in Augusta, Georgia, which they named the Augusta National Golf Club. The course had been designed by Alister MacKenzie and Jones, who had retired from pro golf, and had officially opened the previous year. But Jones wanted to provide an even greater service to his beloved sport. He and Roberts decided to host an annual tournament at the club. Roberts proposed that they call the event the "Masters Tournament," but Jones thought it sounded presumptuous. They settled on the name "Augusta National Invitation Tournament."

The first tournament was held March 22, 1934 (beginning in 1940, the Masters was scheduled each year during the first full week in April). Horton Smith won the first tournament. The name "Augusta National Invitation Tournament" did not last long: By 1939, it was officially changed to the Masters Tournament, as Roberts had originally suggested. The tournament was suspended from 1943–1945, during World War II, so that cattle and turkey could be raised on the grounds to help with the war effort.

The Masters is one of four major championships in men's professional golf tournaments that he did not expect to win. Instead, he used the competitions to prepare for his third Masters appearance. A week before the Masters, Woods was playing a practice round of golf at the Isleworth Country Club, a course near his Florida home. He shot a round of 59—13 shots under par—by executing 2 eagles, 9 birdies, and 2 pars on par-5 holes. When he walked up to the first tee at Augusta on Thursday, April 10, Woods felt ready to try to win the tournament. After the first round he was in fourth place. At the end of the second day, after shooting 66 and 6 under par, he found himself atop the leader board, ahead by 3. He burned the course on the third round, and shot an amazing 65, which gave him a commanding 9-stroke lead.

Going deeper into his "zone" on the final day of the tournament, Woods ended the Masters with a record-breaking 12-stroke victory. Woods set many other records on this early spring weekend, including becoming the youngest champion (21 years, 3 months, 14 days old) at Augusta and the first major

(the others are the U.S. Open, the Open Championship or British Open, and the PGA Championship) and is the first of the four to be played every year. The final round of the Masters always occurs on the second Sunday in April, and unlike the other three major championships, it is always held at the same location—the Augusta National Golf Club. It is part of the PGA Tour, the PGA European Tour, and the Japan Golf Tour. A pro golfer who wins the Masters is automatically invited to play in the other three majors for the next five years and earns a lifetime invitation to the Masters.

In addition to a cash award, the winner of the Masters Tournament traditionally receives a special green jacket, a custom that began in 1949 when Sam Snead won the first of his three Masters titles. The jacket is the official attire worn by Augusta National members while at Augusta National; each Masters winner becomes an honorary member of the club. Winners keep their jacket during the first year after their first win, and then return it to the club to wear when they visit. Part of the green jacket tradition is that the winner of the previous year's Masters put the jacket on the winner after the tournament ends.

champion of black or Asian heritage. Lee Elder was among the many people who celebrated Woods's historic win. Elder said,

> This is so significant sociologically. It's more significant to me, even than Jackie Robinson breaking the [baseball] color line. It's such a great day for golf. It's such a great day for all people. . . . After today, we will have a situation where no one will ever even turn their head to notice when a black person walks to the first tee.

After Woods hugged both of his parents, he headed straight to the clubhouse to tally up his scorecard, sign it, and make it official. Then he walked over to the Butler Cabin for the traditional green jacket ceremony. Nick Faldo, the 1996 Masters Champion, put the Green Jacket on Woods, signifying a new champion of Augusta. Heading back outside, Woods spotted Elder in the crowd and called him over. As the two men embraced, Woods whispered in Elder's ear, "Thanks for making this possible." The man who had once been a toddler who swung cut-down clubs and took a nap after playing golf had realized that dream of being Masters Champion. Almost as if he had transported himself back to that toddler, while everyone ate and celebrated later that evening, Woods was fast asleep in bed, hugging his green jacket.

A PHENOMENAL CAREER

After Woods won the Masters in 1997, he went on to win them three more times, in 2001, 2002, and 2005. In other PGA majors, Woods set a record with his first U.S. Open win in 2000 (he won it again in 2002), and became the first golfer ever to win the U.S. Open, U.S. Amateur, and U.S. Junior Amateur titles. Woods has won the British Open three times in 2000, 2005, and 2006, as well as four PGA Championships in 1999, 2000, 2006, and 2007, which gives him a total of 12 major championships. His hero Jack Nicklaus won 18 championships over the course of his professional career of more than 40 years. Woods sits in second place in total majors wins, and arguably has achieved the Grand Slam of Golf: winning all four majors in a one-year period. Only four other golfers in history have achieved that record. Some would say that it is not a natural Grand Slam because three of his wins came in 2000, and one came in 2001. Others argue that the wins were consecutive, counting the 2001 Masters win as the fourth. For a champion of Woods's caliber, it is irrelevant. By the end of the 2007 season, after being in the pros for 10 years, Woods had won 82 professional tournaments, 61 on the PGA Tour, and had earned a staggering $76,579,376 million, a career money leader on the PGA Tour.

Woods has broken so many records they are almost impossible to catalogue. He has won dozens of Golfer of the Year and Athlete of the Year awards, is a seven-time PGA Tour Vardon Trophy winner, a nine-time PGA Tour Player of the Year, and became the youngest number-one ranked player in the world. His face has adorned dozens and dozens of magazine covers. *Sports Illustrated* selected Woods as their 1996 and 2000 Sportsman of the Year, and the Associated Press chose Woods as the Male Athlete of the Year for 1997, 1999, and 2000.

PASSING ON VALUES

Earl and Kultida Woods brought up a son with strong values. Earl Woods always said he wanted to his son to be a good person. The family motto between father and son—caring and sharing—was never far from Woods's heart no matter how many tournaments he won or how much money he earned. In 1996, Woods and his father established the Tiger Woods Foundation to follow through on that belief through actions and deeds. In his letter to visitors on his Web site, Woods writes:

> From early childhood, I dreamed of being the world's best golfer. I worked hard and applied my family's values to everything I did. Integrity, honesty, discipline, responsibility, and fun: I learned these values at home and in school, each one pushing me further toward my dream.

It was over 10 years ago that my father and I began with the idea of bringing our family motto of "caring and sharing" to the rest of the world. In those days, we traveled the country holding junior golf clinics and encouraging kids to dream big and set specific goals to make those dreams a reality.

Throughout the years, I've had the opportunity to meet thousands of children across the country, and all of them share one common bond: they all dream about their futures. As a result, I learned that success on the course was only part of what I wanted to achieve. In 1996, my father and I established the Tiger Woods Foundation to inspire youth, because I believe in passing on the values I received from my parents and teachers.

I can proudly say more than 10 million young people have been touched by the Tiger Woods Foundation. Through character development programs, scholarships, grants, junior golf teams, and the Tiger Woods Learning Center, the Foundation is helping young people reach their goals.

One of the centerpieces of the Tiger Woods Foundation is the 14-acre Tiger Woods Learning Center (TWLC) in Anaheim, California. The two-story, 35,000-square-foot (3,252-square-meter) facility provides students in fourth through twelfth grades with "free interactive enrichment programs in reading, math, science, and technology. Specific classes promote career exploration and preparation in areas including forensic science, engineering, aerospace, video production and home design." According to Woods, the goal of the learning center is "to provide students with a place to explore their dreams and open doors to new opportunities and potential career paths." The TWLC was dedicated on February 10, 2006. On hand to help with the opening of the center were President Bill Clinton, First Lady of California Maria Shriver, and area students, teachers and community leaders. During the dedication,

Woods said, "This is by far the greatest thing that has ever happened to me. This is bigger than golf. This is bigger than anything I've done on the golf course, because we will be able to shape lives."

Earl Woods had always been a huge proponent of encouraging athletes who have been successful in their sport to give something back. Although he was sick and unable to attend the opening, he told a reporter in an earlier interview, "I hope the message goes out loud and clear that more athletes should give back to the community and give back to the sport that made you what you are today."

LOVE, MARRIAGE, LOSS

In 2001, Swedish golfer Jesper Parnevik changed Woods's life by introducing him to Elin Nordegren, the nanny of Parvenik's four children. Woods and Nordegren began to date, and by the time Woods arrived to play at the 2002 Masters tournament, Elin was accompanying him to most of his events. Woods proposed to Nordegren in November 2003, during a walk at sunset on a game preserve after he finished the President's Cup in South Africa. On October 5, 2004, beneath a multicolored sunset on the island of Barbados, Woods and Nordegren exchanged vows in front of more than 120 guests. Aside from their parents, Earl and Kultida Woods and Thomas Nordegren and Barbro Holmberg (Holmberg, Nordegren's mother, was Sweden's immigration minister), there were also celebrity guests, including Oprah Winfrey, Michael Jordan, and Charles Barkley.

Although Earl Woods was well enough to attend his son's wedding, the years of smoking and neglect had began to take their toll. Woods had survived two open-heart bypass surgeries, had become a diabetic, and was diagnosed with prostate cancer in 1998. He had radiation treatments, but the cancer returned in 2004. The last tournament he had been able to attend to watch his son play was the Target World Challenge

Tiger Woods celebrates with his wife, Elin Nordegren, after winning the eighty-eighth PGA Championship golf tournament at Medinah Country Club on August 20, 2006. Woods met Nordegren while she was the nanny for Swedish golfer Jesper Parnevik's children.

in December 2004. When he finally succumbed to the cancer on May 3, 2006, he was 74 years old. Woods paid tribute to his father on his Web site and withdrew from public view to mourn the loss of his best friend. He attempted to play through his grief at the U.S. Open in June, but his game was not there and he missed the cut for the first time in his professional career. It was a bitter moment for Woods, who had dedicated the Open to his father on that Father's Day weekend, hoping to win it in his memory.

Woods took some additional time off before he walked back onto the golf course at Cog Hill Golf and Country Club in Lemont, Illinois, to play in the Cialis Western Open. He played far better in this July event, using the time on the course as the lead-up for the British Open at the Royal Liverpool Golf Club, in Hoylake, England. Woods was the defending champion and was determined to focus his emotions on the game. In the end, he did what he needed to do and finished the tournament with a 2-shot win over Chris DiMarco, equaling Tom Watson's back-to-back wins in 1982–1983. It was Woods's eleventh major championship, and the first one he could not share with his father. The Associated Press described what happened at the end of his putt on the afternoon of July 23:

> He plucked the ball out of the cup, turned slightly and started to grin when a mixture of sadness and satisfaction washed over his face and he screamed out, "Yes!" Woods buried his head in the shoulder of caddie Steve Williams, sobbing uncontrollably, his chest heaving. Then he found his wife, Elin, and hugged her for the longest minute, tears still streaming down his face. "I'm kind of the one who bottles things up a little bit and moves on," he said. "But at that moment, it just came pouring out. And of all the things that my father has meant to me and the game of golf, I just wish he would have seen it one more time."

Woods went on a tear after the British Open, winning the next four tournaments in a row. After a ninth-place finish in the HSBC World Match Play Championship, he finished out the year with three more wins and two second-place finishes.

Tiger Woods (left) smiles as he stands with (left to right) his daughter Sam, mother Kultida, and wife Elin Nordegren. The bronze statue bearing the likeness of Tiger with his late father, Earl Woods, was unveiled inside the Tiger Woods Learning Center in Anaheim, California, January 21, 2008.

THE TIGER HAS A CUB

On his thirty-first birthday, Woods made the joyous announcement on his Web site that he was going to be a father, "I have always wanted to be a dad. I just wish my father could be around to share the experience." Earl Woods was never far from his son's thoughts. Since the baby was due during the U.S. Open, Woods had made it clear that the birth came first and he would skip the Open if necessary. On Monday, June 18, less than 24 hours after the tournament ended, Woods's daughter, Sam Alexis, was born.

Woods still has plenty of great golf in front of him, and many more records to make. Almost single-handedly, Tiger Woods helped to transform the game of golf because of and in spite of his multiracial heritage. It was not a banner he sought to carry, or a cause he set out to bring to the forefront in the world of golf, it was simply what he was born into. Through forces beyond his control, he made professional golf a more exciting sport. From child prodigy, to teen phenomenon, to manhood, Tiger Woods has always tried to live by the "caring and sharing" motto he and his beloved father followed. If a man's legacy is what he has done with his life, then Tiger Woods will have a great professional one. If a legacy goes beyond personal success, Woods will have succeeded there, as well. It is a legacy passed from father to son, one that his parents gave to him and that he shares with others through his golf clinics, Tiger Woods Foundation, and Tiger Woods Learning Center. There is plenty more that Woods may yet accomplish both on and off the golf course. He has already established a wonderful legacy, one that not only others can appreciate, but one of which his own daughter can be proud. Woods can only hope that what his father passed on to him, he will pass on to his daughter. That will be the greatest gift Tiger can give his father.

1975 Eldrick T. Woods is born on December 30 to Earl and Kultida Woods; nicknamed "Tiger" after his father's friend Vuong Dang Phong, a Vietnamese combat buddy with the same nickname.

1978 Woods, age two, appears on the *Mike Douglas Show.*

1979 Woods, age three, shoots a 48 over 9 holes at the Navy Golf Club in Cypress, California.

1981 He is featured in *Golf Digest* magazine and on the ABC television show *That's Incredible.*

1984 He wins his first Optimist International Junior Championship; will win again in 1985, 1988, 1989, 1990, and 1999.

1990 He is named Southern California Amateur Player of the Year; will win again in 1991.

1991 At 15, Woods becomes the youngest golfer ever to win the U.S. Junior Amateur competition; *Golf Digest* names him Amateur Player of the Year.

1992 Woods defends his title at the U.S. Junior National Championships to become the first to win the title more than once; enters the Nissan Los Angeles Open, his first PGA Tour event, as the youngest player ever to appear in a Tour tournament.

1994 Woods becomes the youngest winner ever to take the U.S. Amateur Championship at the TPC at Sawgrass; enrolls at Stanford University.

1995 He defends his title as U.S. Amateur champion to become the first male since Bobby Jones to win a USGA title in five consecutive years; participates in his first PGA major tournament, the Masters, as the only amateur to make the cut.

1996 Woods becomes the first golfer in history to win three consecutive U.S. Amateur titles; turns pro in August and signs endorsement deals totaling $60 million ($40 million from Nike and $20 million from Titleist); named *Sports Illustrated* Sportsman of the Year; establishes the Tiger Woods Foundation to help fund scholarships throughout the United States, set up clinics, and provide access to golf courses for inner-city children.

1997 Woods becomes the leading money winner on the PGA Tour, with more than $2 million in earnings; wins the Masters to become the youngest Masters winner ever and the first person of Asian or African heritage to win a major tournament.

1998 Woods, in an "off" year, wins only one official PGA event, the BellSouth Classic, to end an 11-tournament winless streak.

1999 He becomes the first golfer in history to earn more than $6 million in one year; wins second PGA major title; records eight PGA victories overall; finishes year with an average of 68.43 strokes, the lowest ever in PGA Tour history.

2000 Woods wins the Mercedes Championship and AT&T Pebble Beach National Pro-Am, his fifth and sixth consecutive PGA Tour victories (the longest streak since Ben Hogan in 1948); becomes fifth player in history (and the youngest ever) to complete career Grand Slam by winning British Open by eight strokes; named *Sports Illustrated*'s Sportsman of the Year for the second time (first person ever to be honored with the award more than once).

2001 Woods wins the Masters tournament and becomes the first golfer to be champion of all four majors simultaneously.

2002 Woods wins second consecutive Masters, his third overall; becomes the youngest golfer in history to win seven PGA majors; is one of only three repeat winners in tournament history (Jack Nicklaus in 1965–1966 and Nick Faldo in 1989–1990 are others); wins his second U.S. Open at Bethpage Black.

2003 Woods comes in first in 5 of 18 tournaments entered, and ends the season winning more than $6.6 million dollars.

2004 Woods becomes the first player to pass the $40 million mark in career earnings; marries Elin Nordegren in Barbados in early October.

2005 Woods becomes one of only three players ever to win four or more Masters (six-time winner Jack Nicklaus and four-time winner Arnold Palmer are other two); wins British Open for second time, his tenth major title; becomes one of only two players (Jack Nicklaus is the other one) to win all four major tournaments at least twice.

2006 Woods's father, Earl Woods, age 74, dies of cancer in early May; in June, Woods fails to make cut for U.S. Open by three strokes, having done so in 39 consecutive majors; wins his third British Open with an 18-under-par score for his eleventh major win; wins Buick Open in August to become youngest player to win 50 PGA tournaments.

2007 Woods ends his PGA Tour winning streak (seven in all) to Nick O'Hern at the Accenture Match Play Championship in Arizona; wins fourth PGA Championship and thirteenth major title at Southern Hills Country Club in Tulsa, Oklahoma; wins third consecutive CA Championship and sixth overall; Sam Alexis Woods, Woods's daughter, is born in Florida in June.

2008 Woods finishes at 19-under 269 to win the Buick Invitational for the fourth consecutive year, the only player to earn such a winning streak at two events (he also won four in a row at Bay Hill), and achieves third-straight PGA Tour victory.

Adams, Mike. *Play Golf for Juniors: The Academy of Golf at PGA National*. Richmond Hill, Ontario: Firefly Books, 2000.

Christopher, Matt. *On the Course with . . . Tiger Woods*, 1st ed. New York: Little, Brown Young Readers, 1998.

Doeden, Matt. *Sports Heroes and Legends: Tiger Woods*. New York: Barnes and Noble/Lerner Publications, 2005.

Edwards, Nicholas. *Tiger Woods: The American Master*. New York: Scholastic, 2001.

Gutman, Bill. *Tiger Woods: A Biography*. New York: Pocket Books, 1997.

Miller, William. *Night Golf*. New York: Lee & Low Books, 2002.

Roberts, Jeremy. *Tiger Woods*, rev. ed. Minneapolis: First Avenue Editions, 2007.

Savage, Jeff. *Amazing Athletes: Tiger Woods*, rev. ed. Minneapolis: First Avenue Edition, 2007.

Stewart, Mark. *Tiger Woods: Drive to Greatness*. Minneapolis: Millbrook Press, 2001.

Strege, John. *Tiger: A Biography of Tiger Woods*. New York: Broadway Books, 1997.

Woods, Earl. *Training a Tiger: A Father's Guide to Raising a Winner in Both Golf and Life*. New York: HarperCollins, 1997.

WEB SITES
Tiger Woods Official Web Site
www.tigerwoods.com

The Official Home of the PGA
http://www.pga.com/home/

Statistics at the Golf Channel
http://www.thegolfchannel.com/statistics/

Judy L. Hasday, a native of Philadelphia, Pennsylvania, earned a B.A. in Communications and an M.Ed in Educational Media from Temple University. Ms. Hasday has worked as a photo editor and freelance writer for more than 25 years. She is a published author of young adult nonfiction; more than 25 of her books are in print. She has won five book awards including three "Best Books for Teens" from the New York Public Library, a National Social Studies Council Book Award, and one from VOYA (Voice of Youth Advocacy). Many of her photographs have been published in books and magazines, with her most recent publication appearing in the Travel Section of the Philadelphia *Inquirer*. Ms Hasday devotes much of her free time to volunteering her photography talents to several non-profit fundraising events for the Greater Delaware Valley Chapter of the Multiple Sclerosis Society and the Philadelphia Chapter of The National Ovarian Cancer Coalition.